Physical Characteristics of the
Bedlington Terrier
(from the American Kennel Club breed standard)

D1482855

Body: Muscular and markedly flexible.

Back: Good natural arch over the loin, creating a definite tuck-up of the underline. Body slightly greater in length than height.

Tail: Set low, scimitar-shaped, thick at the root and tapering to a point which reaches the hock.

Coat: A very distinctive mixture of hard and soft hair standing well out from the skin. Crisp to the touch but not wiry, having a tendency to curl, especially on the head and face.

Height: The preferred Bedlington Terrier dog measures 16.5 inches at the withers, the bitch 15.5 inches.

Weight: To be proportionate to height within the range of 17 to 23 pounds.

Legs and Feet: Lithe and muscular. The hind legs are longer than the forelegs, which are straight and wider apart at the chest than at the feet. Long hare feet with thick, well-closed-up, smooth pads. Dewclaws should be removed.

Bedlington Terrier

By Muriel P. Lee

Contents

KENNEL CLUB BOOKS® **BEDLINGTON TERRIER**
ISBN: 1-59378-296-9

Copyright © 2006 • Kennel Club Books, LLC
308 Main Street, Allenhurst, NJ 07711 USA
Cover Design Patented: US 6,435,559 B2 • Printed in South Korea

Photography by David Dalton, Isabelle Français, Carol Ann Johnson, Karen Taylor, Michael Trafford and Alice van Kempen
with additional photographs by:

Ashbey Photography, Norvia Behling, Mary Bloom, Booth Photography, Paulette Braun, Alan and Sandy Carey, Carolina Biological Supply, Nolan Conley, Cook Photography, Cott/Francis Photography, Dean Photography, Gilbert Photography, Graham Photography, Chris Halvorson, Bill Jonas, Dr. Dennis Kunkel, Tam C. Nguyen, Phototake, Jean Claude Revy and Missy Yuhl.

Illustrations by Rénee Low and Patricia Peters.

The publisher wishes to thank all of the owners whose dogs are illustrated in this book, including Valerie Armstead, Ronnie Armstead-Williams, Capstone Bedlingtons, Shirley Davies, Mary Jo Dunn, Linda Freeman, Lucy Heyman, Candace Sandfort and Peggy M. Schulman.

An English original, the Bedlington Terrier has become known worldwide for its distinct appearance. While beautiful and dainty-looking, the Bedlington is both hardy and agile—a true terrier in "lamb's" clothes!

HISTORY OF THE

BEDLINGTON TERRIER

Have you ever seen a dog being walked on the street by his master and thought, "What is that? It looks like a lamb!" That adorable "lambkin" is the Bedlington Terrier. Although he may look like a lamb, this is a dog that is all terrier, one who has the heart of a lion but is a charming, gentle and first-class companion. Although he is most often now a loyal companion for his family, his original terrier instincts have not been lost. He will be equally at home on a country estate chasing a rabbit or in an apartment lounging about with his owner.

The Bedlington Terrier may not be the dog for everyone, as terriers are active, busy dogs and this dog is no exception. However, if you like a plucky dog, one who fits easily into most any lifestyle, this may be just the one for you.

WHAT IS A TERRIER?
As with that of all terriers, the history of the Bedlington Terrier is a convoluted and difficult road to follow. Edwin Brough wrote in the early 1900s, "He who attempts to discover the origin and trace the history of any one of our

CANIS LUPUS

"Grandma, what big teeth you have!" The gray wolf, a familiar figure in fairy tales and legends, has had its reputation tarnished and its population pummeled over the centuries. Yet it is the descendants of this much-feared creature to which we open our homes and hearts. Our beloved dog, *Canis domesticus*, derives directly from the gray wolf, a highly social canine that lives in elaborately structured packs. In the wild, the gray wolf can range from 60 to 175 pounds, standing between 25 and 40 inches in height.

breeds of dogs, beyond a comparatively few generations, will, in most or all cases, speedily find himself in a fog, tossed on a sea of doubt, driven hither and thither by the conflicting evidence of the writers he consults, who seem to emulate each other in the meagerness of the information they give and the vagueness with which they convey it."

Hoping to defy any sense of the meager and vague, let us begin. The Bedlington Terrier belongs to the classification of dogs described as terriers, from the Latin word *terra*, meaning "earth." The terrier is a dog that has been bred to work beneath the ground to drive out small and large vermin, rodents and other animals that can be a nuisance to country living. Nearly all of the dogs in the Terrier Group originated in the British Isles with the exception of the Australian Terrier, the Cesky Terrier and the American Staffordshire Terrier. Although these breeds do not hail from the British Isles, they were developed from British dogs: the Cesky Terrier from an original cross of the Scottish Terrier and the Sealyham Terrier, the Australian Terrier from a series of crosses of various terrier breeds and the American Staffordshire Terrier from the Staffordshire Bull Terrier.

Many of the terrier breeds were derived from a similar ancestor and, as recently as the mid-1800s, the terriers fell roughly into two basic categories: the rough-coated, short-legged dogs, which tended to come from Scotland, and the longer legged, smooth-coated dogs, which were bred in England. The terriers, although they may differ in type, all have the same character, being game dogs who go to ground after vermin or larger animals.

In 1735, the *Sportsman's Dictionary* described the terrier as a kind of hound, used only or chiefly for hunting the fox or badger. "He creeps into the ground and then nips and bites the fox and badger, either by tearing them in pieces with his teeth, or else hauling them and pulling them by force out of their lurking holes."

The terrier background is obscure, but what is certain is that in the 1700s and early 1800s there was no definite breed of terrier, only dogs that were bred to go to ground with courage and conviction. Those who were unable to do the job were destroyed, and those who could do the proper work were bred to one another with little regard for type. "Unless they were fit and game for the purpose, their heads were not kept long out of the huge butt of water in the stable yard."

Those who bred and kept dogs had a specific purpose of work for their particular breed—long legs for speed, short legs for going to ground and double coats for protection against the elements. Regardless of their intended quarry, all terriers have a powerful set of teeth.

SO DISTINCT, HE'S UNUSUAL

Dog authority and author Will Judy wrote in 1935, "The Bedlington is distinctive in appearance. The deep-sunken eyes of sleepy expression attract the observer, though the same eyes quickly rouse to action. The straggly coat of blue or sandy color, the light build, the sheeplike head and sheeplike coat unite to set him apart as an unusual terrier."

ORIGIN OF THE BEDLINGTON TERRIER

Originally called the Rothbury Terrier, the Bedlington hails from the Border Counties between England and Scotland. This is rocky, hilly country where there is an abundance of wildlife and vermin—ideal terrier country! Also from this area are the Border Terrier, the Dandie Dinmont

In the 1930s, Mr. John Cornforth's Nelson was typical of the Bedlingtons of that period—a dramatic difference from the dogs of today.

A very famous champion at the end of the 19th century was Eng. Ch. Humbleden Blue Boy. Note that the trimming of that time is quite different from that of today. The head shows a stop, which is not apparent in present-day dogs.

Terrier and the Lakeland Terrier. They are all keenly game and natural hunters that have courage and stamina and are able to go to ground after rats, rabbits, foxes, badgers, otters and martens.

Although the Bedlington's background is vague, there are some general assumptions that can be made as far as the Bedlington's roots are concerned. It is assumed that one of the foundation dogs is the Old English Terrier, with crosses to the Otterhound and possibly to the Dandie Dinmont. On occasion, it has been mentioned that the Whippet is also in the Bedlington's background because of the similarity in conformation, including the dog's

head shape, abdominal tuck-up and speed, but, in general, this is refuted by most experts.

A dog by the name of Old Flint, whelped in 1782, is considered to be the progenitor of the modern breed. In the early 1820s, Joseph Aynsley from the town of Bedlington in Northumberland purchased Peachem and bred him to Phoebe, and they produced a son named Piper. Aynsley then acquired a bitch called Cotes Phoebe, who was bred to Anderson's Piper. Thus the breed had its start.

In 1873 the first Stud Book of England's Kennel Club listed 30 Bedlingtons but noted that the majority of them were listed as

"Pedigree not recorded," "Unknown" or "Uncertain," and only 11 had the names of their sires and dams recorded.

Around the early 1900s, not only were better records being kept, but the breed started to be bred as a companion dog and, surprisingly, became a dog who had manners and a taste for luxury. Methods of trimming improved and the dog took on the look of a lovely sheared lamb; however, the heart of a terrier still beat, and the Bedlington has never lost its terrier skills of going after game and vermin.

The first dog show with a class for Bedlingtons was held in Newcastle, England in 1879, with an entry of 52. Mr. Thomas J. Pickett, who was an ardent supporter of the breed, won with his dog Tear 'em. In 1871 Mr. Pickett again won the breed over

A delightful photo showing the young Master Horlick with two of his family's favorite Bedlingtons.

an entry of 22 with a bitch called Tyneside. At the 1873 show Pickett won first place with the bitch Tyne, a sister to Tear 'em. Tear 'em placed second and Tyneside was third. Pickett said that no breed could compare with the Bedlington for stamina, courage and resolution.

Pickett wrote, "I look upon the Bedlington as a farmer's friend and country gentleman's companion. No breed of Terrier can compare with him for stamina, fire, courage and resolution. He will knock about all day with his master, busy as a bee at foxes, rabbits or otters; and at night, when any other sort of dog would be stiff, sore and utterly jaded, he will turn up bright as a new shilling and ready for any game going. He takes to the water readily, has a capital nose, is most intelligent and lively and is a

Miss Lawis, owner of a Bedlington kennel, shown arriving at the 1934 Crufts Show. The dog on the left won a Challenge Certificate.

rough and ready friend about the fields and woods—he has no equal."

Mrs. Maud Mead, of Sudston kennels, purchased a dog named Raggles in 1909 from his breeder, E. Hurley, and remained a supporter, fancier and breeder up until the mid-1930s. She devoted her efforts to the British Bedlington Club, formed in 1910 by Percy Smith. By 1933, however, many of its members had left the club to join the more successful Bedlington Terrier Association, which had been established in 1924.

By 1934, the British Bedlington Club had disbanded due to declining membership. The Sudston Cup, named after Mrs. Mead's kennel, was then transferred to the National Bedlington Terrier Club. Her Sudston Panther was a well-known sire of the area, described by his breeder as "A fine upstanding dog, on the large side, but entirely free from coarseness. An enormously long, fine head, flat, well-placed ears, well-

Bet of Bransways being trimmed by Miss Branfoot.

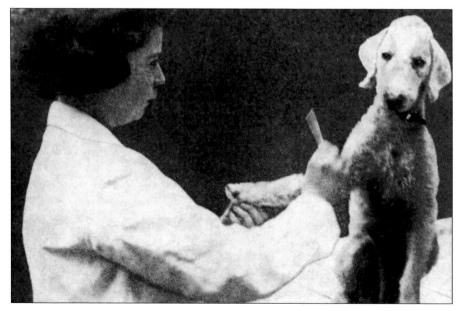

Miss Goodrick, an exhibitor of Bedlingtons during the 1930s, combing out a dog's legs before their appearance in the ring.

set eyes. Perfect front and grand outline." The doggie press critic noted, "Shade big but a wonderful bodied, boned and quartered dog; his blue coat handles well, and he has a long, shapely head; a most likely sire."

THE BEDLINGTON IN THE US

The Bedlington Terrier was exported to the United States in the late 1800s, and the first entry to appear in the American Kennel Club Stud Book was in 1883. The breed was not a particularly popular dog in America, and it took until 1924 for registrations to reach ten per year. However, the breed was somewhat more popular in Canada, where two litters were bred as early as 1883.

The first American championship won by a Bedlington was in 1884 by Ch. Blucher, whelped in England in 1882. By the mid-1880s, a group of fanciers noted that the breed should be taken seriously and wrote the first American standard for the Bedlington. By

Ch. Southwind's Blue Velvet, America's number-one Bedlington in 1969 and 1970 and one of the top-winning terriers in those years as well, handled by Jack Funk under judge Percy Roberts.

The top-winning Bedlington of 1971 and 1972, Ch. Jolee Jingle Bells of Dovern, handled by Joe Waterman.

1900, there were 5 American champions of title, and 70 or so Bedlingtons had been registered. The going price of a pet puppy was $50.00, whereas a show prospect could cost the fantastic sum (for those times) of $500.00.

The Bedlington Terrier in America has been very fortunate, for over the years the breed was supported by several wealthy individuals, and through their efforts the breed remained in the public eye for many years with exceptional winners coming from their kennels. During this period, from about 1920 through the mid-1960s, many exceptional Bedlingtons were whelped and shown in America, compiling wonderful winning records in addition to becoming top producers.

In the early 1900s the breed caught the eye of Col. M. Robert Guggenheim and his Firenze kennels in Long Island, New York. A dog man for years, the colonel had owned over 60 Bulldogs at one time, in addition to a pack of 30 Beagles. He saw the Bedlington Terrier in England around 1905 and eventually imported the best of the Bedlingtons that he could find. Guggenheim had a top kennel man, the Englishman Edward Ward, who traveled the Atlantic on a yearly basis, keeping up on the English Bedlington news and bringing back the best of the breed to Firenze kennels. Between 1920 and 1930, 29

Bedlington champions were made up in America, 23 of which were owned by Firenze kennels.

This trend of importing English greats came to an end within a couple of decades. By 1940, nearly half of the US champions were either bred in America or Canada, whereas prior to this time, 80% of the champions had been imported from England.

Anthony and Anna Neary emigrated from England to the United States in 1929, bringing with them a pair of Bedlingtons called Exiled Laddie and Hasty Morn. Laddie became an American champion and sired six champions. The Nearys were strong supporters of the breed, supporting major Bedlington entries at the Eastern shows. In 1940 they entered the very prestigious Westminster Kennel Club show, and their dog was selected Best American-bred Terrier. William Rockefeller was at this show and later called the Nearys, offering Mr. Neary the position of kennel manager of his Rock Ridge kennels.

The Rockefellers and the Nearys proved to be an unbeatable combination in the US. Numerous champions came out of this kennel for over three decades, up until Mr. Neary's retirement from kennel managing and handling. The outstanding dog from the Rock Ridge kennels was Ch. Rock Ridge Night Rocket, whelped in 1946. For the time, he had one of

GRAND RIVER
KENNEL CLUB

Ch. Ray's Smoky of Rowanoaks in 1971, when he was one of the top dogs in the breed, shown winning a Terrier Group under judge Tom Gannon.

the top show careers of any dog of any breed. At little more than one year of age, he was Best in Show at the prestigious Morris and Essex show, the show held on the grounds of the estate of Mrs. Geraldine Dodge. The next February, he was Best in Show at Westminster Kennel Club and, the following year, he again was Best in Show at the Morris and Essex show. He was used sparingly at stud but in a short and limited career he sired 36 champions. To this day, he remains one of the greats among Bedlington Terriers.

Another American kennel of renown, started in the mid-1930s, was Rowanoaks kennels, owned by Col. and Mrs. P. V. G. Mitchell and their daughter, Connie Willemsen. The Mitchells traveled to England and imported two outstanding dogs: Ch. Tarragona of Rowanoaks and Ch. Love Letter. Tarragona went to the top in the show ring, in addition to siring 23 champions. However, within a year, his daughter, Ch. Lady Rowena of Rowanoaks, bested him in the ring, winning an all-breed Best in Show in 1938 while still in the Puppy

Class. In 1939 she won Best in Show at the well-known American terrier show held by the Montgomery County Kennel Club.

The Mitchells, very active in the breed for many years, bred for correct breed type, beautiful heads and proper coats. They never kept more than 12 dogs and finished over 100 champions. They were active until the late 1960s and their daughter, Mrs. Willemsen, was also very active in the Bedlington Terrier Club of America.

In America, by the 1950s and 1960s, many new breeders became active, producing more notable dogs. Martha McVay of Marvay kennels in California has been active for nearly half a century. Dogs from her kennel have had many Terrier Group placements through the years, in addition to winning the national speciality six times.

Milo and Marjorie Hanson from California and their Valgo kennels produced over 75 champions and also earned obedience degrees on several more. Center Ridge kennels in Milwaukee, Wisconsin finished 30 champions. Ch. Center Ridge Snow Classic, whelped in 1955, won 5 Bests in Show and 40 Group Firsts. Am./Can. Ch. Center Ridge Minute Man had two Bests in Show and sired nine champion get. Am./Can. Ch. Center Ridge Lady Caroline, whelped in 1959, won 15 Bests in Show and 62 Group Firsts and still had time to produce 2 champion get.

In 1948, 218 Bedlingtons were registered in the US and, by 1958, registrations had more than doubled to 573. By 1968, registrations had risen to 778.

Mrs. Marian Cabage from Illinois was active in the 1960s, and her most well-known dog was Ch. Southwind's Blue Velvet, the top terrier in 1969 and also recipient of the *Kennel Review* Award for that year. He retired with 18 Bests in Show and 125 Group Firsts, having sired 32 champions.

David Ramsey of Willow Wind kennels was the Bedlington breeder who made the greatest impact on the breed during the last quarter of the 20th century. Ch. Willow Wind Silver Cloud, sire of 15 champions, was the top

An early winner, Ch. Van-Dee's Snocap of Valgo.

Bedlington sire in 1980. His double-granddaughter was the top Bedlington in 1983. Mr. Ramsey's greatest dog was Ch. Willow Wind Centurian. At the Beverly Hills show, Centurian defeated 700 terriers to win the Terrier Group. In the 1990s, Ch. Willow Wind Play It My Way was a multi-Best in Show dog. Ch. Willow Wind Tenure was the top terrier in 1999.

In the United States the Bedlington has remained fairly popular. The breed has been fortunate to have some exceptional owners over the years who have been interested in having their dogs campaigned; these dogs have made the breed memorable, even though the breed's numbers have been relatively small. Currently the breed ranks in the lower third in registrations of AKC-recognized breeds.

Jackie Fogel, from West Bend, Wisconsin, has been breeding Bedlingtons since the early 1990s under the First Class prefix. Ch. First Class the Euro (or "JR") won Best of Breed at the Westminster Kennel Club show twice, was a national specialty winner and number-one Bedlington, all systems, in 2002. JR is now living in France, providing tough competition to the European Bedlingtons. Two of his French puppies have returned to the US to gain their American championships. JR's dam was Ch. Willow Wind It's My

The top Bedlington Terrier for five years in the mid/late 1980s, Ch. Willow Wind Centurian, owner/breeder-handled by David Ramsey to Best in Show at Spring-field Kennel Club in 1986 under judge Pete Dawkins.

Party, winner of the Top Producer of the Year award from the Bedlington Terrier Club of America in 2003. In 2004, four of the top ten Bedlingtons were out of First Class dogs. One of Jackie's biggest thrills was piloting Ch. First Class Superman to Best of Breed at Westminster—the kennel's third

The top Bedlington winner at the turn of the century, Ch. Willow Wind Tenure was the number one of all terriers in 2000, winning 27 Bests in Show that year alone. He was handled by Taffe McFadden, shown here with judge Adelene Pardo.

win at Westminster but the first with Jackie handling her own dog. Over 20 champions have come out of the First Class kennels.

Lucy Heyman, from Spring, Texas, has been breeding under the Carillon prefix for many years. As with many breeders, Lucy started with a Bedlington bitch brought home to be the family pet. Another bitch was added to the family who eventually became Ch. Claremont Luna, finishing her championship with multiple Group placements. Luna has numerous champion descendants. To date the kennel claims over 110 Bedlington Terrier champions, including many Group-placing and -winning dogs and national and regional specialty winners. The kennel can claim 5 top producers, including the top dam of all time, Ch. Carillon Salsa Serendipity, dam of 16 champions. In addition, the other top producers are Ch. Carillon Serendipity, dam of Salsa, with 8 champions to her credit; Serendipity's son, Ch. Carillon Boulevardier, sire of 29 champions; and a Serendipity daughter, Ch. Carillon Serendipity Calypso, with 10 champions to her credit. In addition, another son of Serendipity, Ch. Carillon Fuzzi Logic, has 19 champions to date. One of the kennel's top goals is to breed healthy dogs and continue to improve the overall health of the Bedlington Terrier. Over 100 Carillon dogs are listed on the OFA (Orthopedic Foundation for

Animals) website as being free of the various defects and diseases known to affect the breed. Lucy has served on the board of the parent club and serves on the AKC's President's Council of the Canine Health Foundation.

The future of the Bedlington Terrier looks bright with a group of promising breeders who are making significant achievements. On the West Coast, Darlene Swenson Smith has emerged from almost two decades of inactivity to reinvent her successful breeding program with frozen semen saved from the son of her homebred Best in Show winner Ch. Tiffanies Tickle Your Butzky. Dick and Kay Kraft have launched a successful breeding program with their Best in Show, Group-winning and national specialty-winning Ch. Silvery Moon Unforgettable, who also placed second in the Terrier Group at the Westminster Kennel Club show. From San Jose, California, Batyah Taban, well known for her top-winning Afghan Hounds, started her DeHayyim Bedlington-breeding program in the late 1990s and has already produced two Best in Show dogs and several regional specialty winners. In Denver, Dennis and Kristy Corash are producing Group and national specialty winners under their Bonny Brook prefix, along with having a top junior handler in the family, daughter Melissa. Sandra

A group of handsome Bedlingtons with their mistresses.

Bethea, of Mississippi, with little breeding has done well with her dogs in conformation, obedience and agility trials. Harriet Whitbread in Virginia had the top dog in 2004, Ch. Angel's Blue Elvis of Eden, and Linda Freeman, also from Virginia, has had a past Group-winning Pedigree Award winner. Both women are actively breeding Bedlingtons.

THE BEDLINGTON IN MODERN BRITAIN

The Rathsrigg kennel of Ian and Margaret Phillips, West Yorkshire, was established in 1957. Mr. Phillips has certainly been a force in the breed in the UK. Over the years, they have bred about 25 English champions in addition to selling dogs throughout Europe and North America. Mr. Phillips is president of the National Bedlington Terrier Club and has

written an extensive book, *The Centenary Book of the National Bedlington Terrier Club, 1989-1998*, which is available from either Mr. Phillips or from the club.

Notable British breeders have included Mrs. P. Hall of Dalip Bedlingtons. She bred and co-owned, with Mrs. P. Morton, Ch. Dalip Lord of the Rings, who was the top Bedlington and the top sire of 2000, winning a total of 19 Challenge Certificates (CCs, awards toward an English championship) and 14 Bests of Breed, in addition to winning 2 Terrier Groups by the end of 2000.

Mr. and Mrs. R. North own Niddvale Spring Warrior, the Best of Breed winner at the Crufts Dog Show in 2000. Toffset Tiptop, owned by Mr. and Mrs. Wright, won the bitch CC and Best of Breed at the 2000 Welsh Kennel Club show. Mrs. B. F. Emsley

BREED CLUBS

There are two very active clubs for the Bedlington Terrier. In the United Kingdom it is the National Bedlington Terrier Club, and in the US it is the Bedlington Terrier Club of America. In America there are two affiliated clubs, the Bedlington Terrier Club of Greater Chicago and the Bedlington Terrier Club of the West. For information on either national club, contact The Kennel Club (UK) or the American Kennel Club, or check them out online. For further information on breeders, the national club in your country should be contacted.

owned Ch. Hilldyke Alicia, who was Best of Breed at the National Terrier show and top Bedlington bitch in 2000. Mrs. Emsley is secretary/treasurer of the National Bedlington Terrier Club, which publishes the very informative *The Sporting Bedlington*, published twice a year.

At a recent Crufts Dog Show, 80 Bedlington Terriers were entered, which placed the breed numerically about in the middle of terrier entries, but far below the more popular terrier breeds.

BEDLINGTONS AROUND THE WORLD

In Canada the Bedlington Terrier has remained somewhat of an uncommon breed, and its fanciers usually show their dogs in both Canada and the United States. Well-known breeders since the 1960s have been Shirley and Don Martin of the Siwash kennels in Ontario and the Boulevardier kennels of M. Gail Gates and Art Perkins from Saskatchewan. From the Siwash kennels, all dogs owner-handled, came numerous top winners. Ch. Siwash Blue Kelley was second top terrier in 1983 and third top terrier in 1984, won 3 Bests in Show and 27 Group firsts and was Best of Opposite Sex at Montgomery County Kennel Club in 1990 at the age of 9. Ch. Marvay's Melissa of Siwash was the number-four terrier in 1978 and had three all-breed Bests in Show. Ch. Siwash Merry Martin was the number-one Bedlington in Canada in 1989, with multiple Group placements. In 1988, *Dogs in Canada* listed the top 5 dogs in each breed for the previous 25 years, and 4 of the 5 Bedlingtons were from the Siwash kennel.

Boulevardier Bedlingtons, since 1987, have held the number-one Bedlington in Canada position for four different years with four different dogs. Ch. Boulevardier Seltine Tiere was the number-three Bedlington in 1994 and number-two Bedlington in 1995, as well as the number-eight Bedlington in the US. Ch. Boulevardier Bad LeRoy Brown, owned by Elmer Grieve, was the number-one Bedlington in 1994. Ch. Trout on a Line finished his championship with four consecutive Group placements. The motto for this kennel is: "In search of excellence in conformation, temperament and health equally important."

Angela Roper of Nosehill kennels, of Alberta, should also be mentioned. Her Ch. Lady Alexander of Nosehill was Best in Show at the Alberta Kennel Club in 1989. Ms. Roper has been active in obedience, pet therapy and agility training.

In Finland there has been interest in the breed since the 1960s, with some fine kennels breeding and importing winning dogs. Peggen, Hjordie and Erkki Tenlenius of Eho kennels have been well-known for many years, especially for Int. Ch. Leasowes Damask Rose, Best in Show winner at the Helsinki International show in 1964. Int. Ch. Jessica, bred by Mr. Ilpo Malmioja, was best terrier in 1975. Ms. Ritva Kohijoki of Kisapirtin kennels has been well-known for her great winners; of note are Int. Ch. Kisapirtin Perro, Int. Ch. Kisapirtin Miramari, Int. Ch. Kisapirtin Talita and Int. Ch. Kisapirtin Perella. Over the years she has had 12 International Championships, 37 Finnish Championships and about 120 CACIBs (International Champion of Beauty certificates awarded by the Fédération Cynologique Internationale). Registration numbers are small, but the breed

has a devoted following and is able to hold its own at the shows.

The breed is not very popular in New Zealand, and by far the most active breeder is Linda Strongman, who purchased Aust./NZ Ch. Southridge Royal Blue. This dog had won several Australian Bests in Show before being exported to New Zealand, where he has been a Group winner as well as Reserve Best in Show several times. Ms. Strongman has imported several more dogs from Australia and bred NZ Ch. Lynmar Truffels, who has won many awards in New Zealand.

The UK has one of the world's most active Bedlington Terrier breed clubs. Here a Bedlington is exhibited at an outdoor show in England.

CHARACTERISTICS OF THE
BEDLINGTON TERRIER

PERSONALITY

The Bedlington Terrier is a versatile dog and a great house dog and companion. If you like to work with your dog, you will find this breed to be a happy and willing participant in whatever area you choose, be it obedience work, agility, therapy, flyball and, of course, best of all, going-to-ground activities. This is a smart dog that likes to please, to keep busy and to be challenged. Give him any job that requires a bit of brain activity on his part and he will be absolutely delighted. Of course, because of his intelligence, it is best to establish very early on who is the head of the household, and teaching the very basics in obedience lessons is always a good idea.

The Bedlington is a well-loved family dog, giving much and asking little in return. He likes to have appropriate attention from the family and in return will

The Bedlington is an active, hardy, long-lived companion who can make himself at home almost anywhere. This senior is still "sitting pretty" at 12 years of age.

give of himself and be a loving, contributing member of the family. He will be extremely loyal and is very good with children. However, in spite of his lamb-like appearance and soft looks, this is an athletic breed that is every inch a terrier. This is not a breed that will while away the hours quietly on your lap; rather, he will be curious and enthusiastic. He loves to play and entertain, and he will be a great companion dog. He is a good watchdog but is not a noisy breed, barking only when strangers come to the house. He is lively and inquisitive, and you will find him a delight to have with you.

Given his small size, he is a good city dog who not only remains quiet but also requires little space in an apartment. Unlike many other dogs, he does not shed, but he does require weekly coat care.

If you are a first-time dog owner, you must be aware of your responsibility toward your new friend—either keep your dog on a leash or in your fenced yard. Your Bedlington, if loose and trotting along at your side, might spot a squirrel across a busy street. His killer terrier instincts will react quickly and, oblivious of the traffic, he will dart across the street. Therefore some rudimentary obedience training should be in line so your pal will sit when asked to, come when

PART OF THE FAMILY
Bedlington Terriers thrive in organized activities and love to be a part of the family—going for rides in the car, fetching a ball, helping in the kitchen by keeping the floor clean and then cuddling up on the bed when day is done.

called and, in general, act like a gentleman.

Bedlingtons, as with other terriers, can be a challenge in the obedience ring. Terriers are not easy breeds to work with in obedience, as with their intelligence and independent spirit they can sometimes be more trying to train than had been anticipated. You will see Golden Retrievers, Poodles and Miniature Schnauzers in abundance in obedience classes, as these are breeds with which it is easier to work. Not only are these breeds intelligent but, more importantly, they have an eagerness to please their masters, a trait that is not found in abundance in the terrier breeds.

The Bedlington is prized for his wonderful companion qualities as well as his beauty and elegance. This is Ch. Carillon Serendipity Bluenote, owned by Cynthia Cook Pruitt and Paul Pruitt.

PET-LOVER STATS

- 94% of dog owners keep a pet's photo on display in their home or office.
- 46% of dogs sleep on their owners' beds.
- 63% of us celebrate our dogs' birthdays.
- 66% of us take our dogs to the vet more often than we see our own physicians!

The terrier is easily distracted and busy, but he is an intelligent dog and he does respond to training. Of course, when training a smart and independent dog, the handler will often learn humility while the dog is learning sit and stay. The Bedlington is a quick, alert and smart little dog who likes his owner to be his equal.

COAT-CARE REQUIREMENTS

The Bedlington Terrier is a dog that will require weekly grooming, whether you are going to show the dog or just have him as a pet. If you are going to show your dog, a reputable breeder who also shows his animals will be a good source of grooming advice. He will be able to show you how to clip your dog into the proper show trim, and he will also assist you with the finer points of grooming this breed.

If you are buying your Bedlington to be a pet, you will be able to do the trimming yourself (or have the dog professionally

The Bedlington has a non-shedding coat, which, however, does require the removal of dead hair. Left untended, the coat will become matted and eventually smelly, and your dear pet will not be so nice to be around. A weekly or twice-weekly combing will take out the dead hair, making it unlikely that your Bedlington will develop a matted coat. Trimming, whether you have a show dog or a pet, will be required, but you will find it a fairly easy job to keep your dog in pet trim.

Playful, intelligent and curious, the Bedlington wants nothing more than to be part of his owner's life.

groomed) and, as time goes on, you will become as good a groomer of the breed as a professional dog groomer! There are several books on grooming dogs in general, and many Bedlington clubs have breed-specific grooming manuals for sale.

Do understand before purchasing your Bedlington Terrier that this is a breed with a coat that needs maintenance, whether you have a dog for the show ring or one that is a household pet. Keep your dog clean and trimmed and you will find it a pleasure to be in his company. However, it will require some effort to do this.

LIVING WITH A TERRIER

Bryan Cummins wrote, "Terriers, created to hunt down and kill vermin, should all be sold with their own leather jackets. They are often feisty, lively, self-assured. You live with terriers, you do not own them."

Part of the pleasure of owning a Bedlington is pampering him with attentive grooming. Starting when your puppy is young will help him become accustomed to grooming and will give you lots of time to practice.

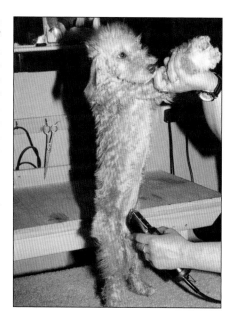

HEALTH CONSIDERATIONS

By and large, Bedlington Terriers are very healthy dogs, as are most other terriers, and there are few health problems in the breed. Your most sensible option is to buy your puppy from a reputable breeder and ask for documentation on any health problems in his line and current health-testing results. Breeding stock should be tested regularly for eye and heart disease, as well as hereditary orthopedic problems, and certified as free of these disorders.

When buying a Bedlington Terrier, you must also be aware that there is one significant health problem in the breed. You must ask the breeder of your dog if he is aware of the problem and has had his dogs tested. This problem is copper toxicosis (CT), which is a serious disease found in some Bedlington Terriers. This is an autosomal recessive disorder of copper accumulation that results in severe liver disease. It is a hereditary condition and one that cannot be ignored. At the present time, considerable research and study are being conducted.

When buying your puppy, be sure to ask the breeder to see the biopsied "normal" certificates or DNA typing of both the sire and the dam. All responsible Bedlington breeders will have their dogs certified "normal" before breeding them. It is thought that the disease may be present in as much as 50% of the breed; however, there was a time when two-thirds of the breed was affected. Some dogs carry the CT gene but are not affected by the disease; this also turns up through DNA typing. If your dog is tested as having the disease, there are now several therapies whereby the dog can be treated and often live a long and full life.

Although this health problem may look daunting, Bedlingtons are considered to be a very healthy breed. The problem mentioned exists in the breed, and a buyer should be aware of it. Do not be turned away from the breed, and do realize that if the breeder of your puppy is reputable and aware, he will be doing his utmost to breed healthy dogs.

Go team! These two football fans are all dressed up and ready for the big game.

This is what a properly groomed Bedlington in show trim should look like. A dog kept in pet trim will require regular grooming as well, though it will not be as extensive.

BREED STANDARD FOR THE

BEDLINGTON TERRIER

As breeders started exhibiting at dog shows, it was realized that there must be more uniformity within each breed; i.e., all puppies in a litter should look similar as well as be of the same type as their sire and dam. Each breed approved by the American Kennel Club has a standard that gives the reader a mental picture of what the specific breed should look like. All reputable breeders strive to produce animals that will meet the requirements of the standard.

Many breeds were developed for a specific purpose, i.e., hunting, retrieving, going to ground, coursing, guarding, herding, etc. The terriers were all bred to go to ground and to pursue vermin. In

The breed's desired conformation, as set forth in the standard, is illustrated beautifully by this fine champion.

addition to having a dog that looks like a proper Bedlington Terrier, the standard assures that he will have the personality, disposition and intelligence that are sought after in the breed. Standards were originally written by fanciers who had a love and a concern for the breed. They knew that the essential characteristics of the Bedlington Terrier were unlike those of any other breed and that care must be taken so that these characteristics were maintained through the generations.

As time progressed and breeders became more aware that certain points of the dog needed a better description or more definition, breeders would meet together and work out a new standard. However, standards for any breed are never changed on a whim, and serious study and exchange between breeders take place before any move is made.

Ch. Claremont Anchor Man, shown winning Best in Show at Ft. Lauderdale Dog Club under judge Judith Fellton in 1981. Anchor Man was one of the top Bedlingtons in the US that year.

LATHY AND LINTY

In the Bedlington lexicon, "lathy" means hard and muscular, supple and tough but not stiff or inactive. The flat ribs give the elbows freedom of movement. "Linty" refers to a particular feature of the coat that only the Bedlington has. The coat is not harsh and it is not soft. It forms a pile that stands out from the skin, is crisp to the touch and has a spring to its texture.

THE AMERICAN KENNEL CLUB BREED STANDARD FOR THE BEDLINGTON TERRIER

GENERAL APPEARANCE

A graceful, lithe, well-balanced dog with no sign of coarseness, weakness or shelliness. In repose the expression is mild and gentle, not shy or nervous. Aroused, the dog is particularly alert and full of immense energy and courage. Noteworthy for endurance, Bedlingtons also gallop at great speed, as their body outline clearly shows.

BETTER THAN THE AVERAGE DOG

Even though you may never show your dog, you should still read the breed standard. The breed standard tells you more than just physical specifications such as how tall your dog should be; it also describes how he should act, how he should move and what unique qualities make him the breed that he is. You are not investing money in a pure-bred dog so that you can own a dog that "sort of looks like" the breed you're purchasing. You want a typical, handsome representative of the breed, one that all of your friends and family and people you meet out in public will recognize as the breed you've so carefully selected and researched. If the parents of your prospective puppy bear little or no resemblance to the dog described in the breed standard, you should keep searching!

HEAD

Narrow, but deep and rounded. Shorter in skull and longer in jaw. Covered with a profuse topknot which is lighter than the color of the body, highest at the crown and tapering gradually to just back of the nose. There must be no stop and the unbroken line from crown to nose end reveals a slender head without cheekiness or snipiness. Lips are black in the blue and blue and tans and brown in all other solid and bi-colors. *Eyes*—Almond-shaped, small, bright and well sunk with no tendency to tear or water. Set is oblique and fairly high on the head. Blues have dark eyes; blues and tans, less dark with amber lights; sandies, sandies and tans, light hazel; livers, livers and tans, slightly darker. Eye rims are black in the blue and blue and tans and brown in all other solid and bi-colors. *Ears*—Triangular with rounded tips. Set on low and hanging flat to the cheek in front with a slight projection at the base. Point of greatest width approximately 3 inches. Ear tips reach the corners of the mouth. Thin and velvety in texture, covered with fine hair forming a small silky tassel at the tip. *Nose*—Nostrils large and well defined. Blues and blues and tans have black noses. Livers, livers and tans, sandies, sandies and tans have brown noses. *Jaws*—Long and tapering. Strong muzzle well filled up with bone beneath the eye. Close-fitting lips, no flews. *Teeth*—Large, strong and white. Level or scissors bite. Lower canines clasp the outer surface of the upper gum just in front of the upper canines. Upper premolars and molars lie outside those of the lower jaw.

NECK AND SHOULDERS

Long, tapering neck with no throatiness, deep at the base and rising well up from the shoulders which are flat and sloping with no excessive musculature. The head is carried high.

BODY

Muscular and markedly flexible. Chest deep. Flat-ribbed and deep through the brisket, which reaches to the elbows. Back has a good natural arch over the loin, creating a definite tuck-up of the underline. Body slightly greater in length than height. Well-muscled quarters are also fine and graceful.

LEGS AND FEET

Lithe and muscular. The hind legs are longer than the forelegs, which are straight and wider apart at the chest than at the feet. Slight bend to pasterns which are long and sloping without weakness. Stifles well angulated. Hocks strong and well let down, turning neither in nor out. Long hare feet with thick, well-closed-up,

Head study of a champion Bedlington, showing both proper structure and proper grooming.

smooth pads. Dewclaws should be removed.

COAT

A very distinctive mixture of hard and soft hair standing well out from the skin. Crisp to the touch but not wiry, having a tendency to curl, especially on the head and face. When in show trim must not exceed 1 inch on body; hair on legs is slightly longer.

TAIL

Set low, scimitar-shaped, thick at the root and tapering to a point which reaches the hock. Not carried over the back or tight to the underbody.

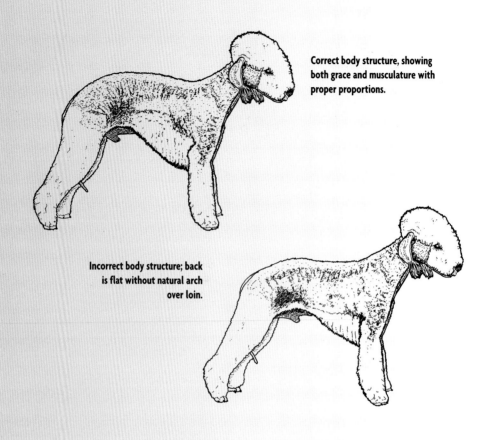

Correct body structure, showing both grace and musculature with proper proportions.

Incorrect body structure; back is flat without natural arch over loin.

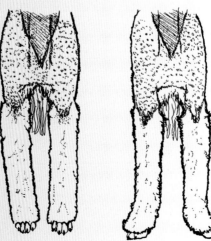

Correct forequarters; legs straight and strong, wider apart at chest than at feet.

Incorrect forequarters; wider at feet than at chest and toeing out.

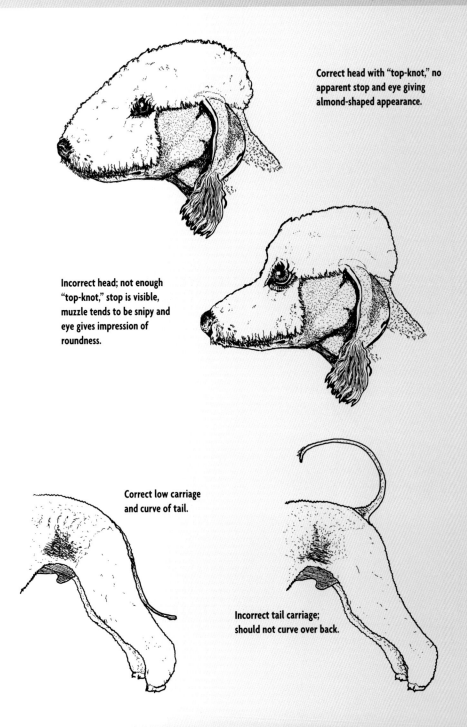

Correct head with "top-knot," no apparent stop and eye giving almond-shaped appearance.

Incorrect head; not enough "top-knot," stop is visible, muzzle tends to be snipy and eye gives impression of roundness.

Correct low carriage and curve of tail.

Incorrect tail carriage; should not curve over back.

BREEDING FOR DOLLARS?

Are you thinking about breeding your bitch so that you can make a quick, easy profit by selling the puppies? Why not? You know that raising a litter is no work at all—the dogs take care of themselves! *Stop right there.* Before you start building that whelping box, let reality be your roadblock.

There is no money in breeding dogs. Consider the costs involved: the bitch's maintenance and special care; the food, formula and veterinary bills for the dam and her pups; the equipment needed to convert part of your home into a kennel, etc. Once you've paid for these things (and there's more!), you wouldn't break even were you to get top dollar for every puppy, which you won't! If you're looking to make money, get a real estate license, become a professional caterer, sell your kid's toys or grandmother's china on eBay®— something along those lines. Any of those ventures will prove more profitable, and then you'll have more money to spend on your canine best friend.

COLOR

Blue, sandy, liver, blue and tan, sandy and tan, liver and tan. In bi-colors the tan markings are found on the legs, chest, under the tail, inside the hindquarters and over each eye. The topknots of all adults should be lighter than the body color. Patches of darker hair from an injury are not objectionable, as these are only temporary. Darker body pigmentation of all colors is to be encouraged.

HEIGHT

The preferred Bedlington Terrier dog measures 16.5 inches at the withers, the bitch 15.5 inches. Under 16 inches or over 17.5 inches for dogs and under 15 inches or over 16.5 inches for bitches are serious faults. Only where comparative superiority of a specimen outside these ranges clearly justifies it, should greater latitude be taken.

WEIGHT

To be proportionate to height within the range of 17 to 23 pounds.

GAIT

Unique lightness of movement. Springy in the slower paces, not stilted or hackneyed. Must not cross, weave or paddle.

APPROVED SEPTEMBER 12, 1967

Handlers should be thoroughly familiar with the breed standard so that they understand what judges are looking for and can present their dogs in the best possible way. The standard is the measuring stick by which show dogs are judged.

BEDLINGTON TERRIER

WHERE TO BEGIN

If you are convinced that the Bedlington Terrier is the ideal dog for you, it's time to learn about where to find a puppy and what to look for. Locating a litter of Bedlington Terriers will require some homework on your part, as the breed is not too numerous. You should inquire about breeders who enjoy a good reputation in the breed. New owners should have as many questions as they have doubts. An established breeder is indeed the one to answer your four million questions and make you comfortable with your choice of the Bedlington Terrier.

When choosing a breeder, reputation is much more important than convenience of location. Fortunately, the majority of Bedlington Terrier breeders are devoted to the breed and its well-being. New owners should have little problem finding a reputable breeder who doesn't live on the other side of the country. The Bedlington Terrier Club of America is a trusted source and can refer prospective owners to responsible member breeders across the US.

Potential owners are encouraged to attend dog shows to see the Bedlington Terriers in action, to meet the owners and handlers firsthand and to get an idea of what this "darling little lamb" looks like outside a photographer's lens. Provided you approach the handlers when they are not busy with the dogs, most are more than willing to answer

COLOR CHANGES

Bedlington puppies are born either black, dark brown or chocolate and will turn to their adult color by one year of age. The American standard phrases the colors thusly: blue, sandy, liver, blue and tan, sandy and tan or liver and tan. The English standard gives the colors of the breed as blue, liver or sandy with or without tan.

questions, recommend breeders and give advice.

Once you have contacted and met a breeder or two and made your choice about which breeder is best suited to your needs, it's time to visit the litter. Keep in mind that many top breeders have waiting lists. Sometimes new owners have to wait a year or longer for a puppy. If you are really committed to the breeder whom you've selected, then you will wait (and hope for an early arrival!).

Since you are likely to be choosing a Bedlington Terrier as a pet dog and not a show dog, you simply should select a pup that is friendly, attractive and healthy. The breeder should be happy to show you health-testing documentation on the litter's parents and should offer some type of health guarantee on his pups. Bedlington Terriers generally have small litters, averaging three or four puppies, so selection is limited once you have located a desirable litter. When considering the sex of your puppy, you should know that male Bedlingtons tend to be more aggressive than females when it comes to meeting other dogs. This is a natural terrier trait that should be considered when selecting a pup. Always check the bite of your selected puppy to be sure that it is neither overshot nor undershot.

Breeders commonly allow visitors to see their litters by

MAKE A COMMITMENT
Dogs are most assuredly man's best friend, but they are also a lot of work. When you add a puppy to your family, you also are adding to your daily responsibilities for years to come. Dogs need more than just food, water and a place to sleep. They also require training (which can be ongoing throughout the lifetime of the dog), activity to keep them physically and mentally fit, hands-on attention every day and grooming and healthcare. Your life as you now know it may well disappear! Are you prepared for such drastic changes?

around the fifth or sixth week, and puppies leave for their new homes between the eighth and tenth week. Breeders who permit their puppies to leave early are more interested in a profit than in their puppies' well-being. Puppies need to learn the rules of the pack from their dams, and most dams continue teaching the pups

one that may fit nicely into your family and lifestyle. If you have researched breeders, you should be able to recognize a knowledgeable and responsible Bedlington Terrier breeder who cares not only about his pups but also about what kind of owner you will be. If you have completed the final step in your new journey, you have found a litter, or possibly two, of quality Bedlington Terrier pups.

A visit with the puppies and their breeder should be an education in itself. Breed research, breeder selection and puppy visitation are very important aspects of finding the puppy of your dreams. Beyond that, these things also lay the foundation for a successful future with your pup. Puppy personalities within each litter vary, from the shy and easy-going puppy to the one who is dominant and assertive, with

While your puppy may not be a piano virtuoso, he will certainly be a first-class snooper! All puppies are curious, but this trait is especially prevalent in the Bedlington Terrier, who wants to learn everything about his surroundings.

manners and dos and don'ts until around the eighth week. Breeders spend significant amounts of time with the Bedlington Terrier toddlers so that the pups are able to interact with the "other species," i.e., humans. Given the long history that dogs and humans have, bonding between the two species is natural but must be nurtured. A well-bred, well-socialized Bedlington Terrier pup wants nothing more than to be near you and please you.

A COMMITTED NEW OWNER

By now you should understand what makes the Bedlington Terrier a most unique and special dog,

most pups falling somewhere in between. By spending time with the puppies you will be able to recognize certain behaviors and what these behaviors indicate about each pup's temperament. Which type of pup will complement your family dynamics is best determined by observing the puppies in action within their "pack." Your breeder's expertise and recommendations are also valuable. Although you may fall in love with a bold and brassy male, the breeder may suggest that another pup would be best for you. The breeder's experience in rearing Bedlington Terrier pups and matching their temperaments with appropriate humans offers the best assurance that your pup will meet your needs and expectations. The type of puppy that you select is just as important as your decision that

SIGNS OF A HEALTHY PUPPY

Healthy puppies are robust little fellows who are alert and active, sporting shiny coats and supple skin. They should not appear lethargic, bloated or pot-bellied, nor should they have flaky skin or runny or crusted eyes or noses. Their stools should be firm and well formed, with no evidence of blood or mucus.

the Bedlington Terrier is the breed for you.

The decision to live with a Bedlington Terrier is a serious commitment and not one to be taken lightly. This puppy is a living sentient being that will be dependent on you for basic survival for his entire life. Beyond the basics of survival—food, water, shelter and protection—he needs much, much more. The new pup needs love, nurturing

You should take time in selecting your Bedlington Terrier puppy. Much can be learned about each pup's personality by watching the littermates interact with each other.

It won't be difficult to find a friendly, attractive puppy from this basket of wee Bedlingtons. Be sensible, however, and not sentimental in choosing your future companion.

This adorable puppy, Skittles Hap, affectionately called "The Little Boss," is pictured at almost four months of age.

YOUR BEDLINGTON TERRIER SHOPPING LIST

Just as expectant parents prepare a nursery for their baby, so should you ready your home for the arrival of your Bedlington Terrier pup. If you have the necessary puppy supplies purchased and in place before he comes home, it will ease the puppy's transition from the warmth and familiarity of his mom and littermates to the brand-new environment of his new home and human family. You will be too busy to stock up and prepare your house after your pup comes home, that's for sure! Imagine how a pup must feel upon being transported to a strange new place. It's up to you to comfort him and to let your little pup know that he is going to be happy with you.

and a proper canine education to mold him into a responsible, well-behaved canine citizen. Your Bedlington Terrier's health and good manners will need consistent monitoring and regular "tune-ups," so your job as a responsible dog owner will be ongoing throughout every stage of his life. If you are not prepared to accept these responsibilities and commit to them for at least the next decade, likely longer, then you are not prepared to own a dog of any breed.

Although the responsibilities of owning a dog may at times tax your patience, the joy of living with your Bedlington Terrier far outweighs the workload, and a well-mannered adult dog is worth your time and effort. Before your very eyes, your new charge will grow up to be your most loyal friend!

PEDIGREE VS. REGISTRATION CERTIFICATE

Too often new owners are confused between these two important documents. Your puppy's pedigree, essentially a family tree, is a written record of a dog's genealogy of three generations or more. The pedigree will show you the names as well as performance titles of all dogs in your pup's background. Your breeder must provide you with a registration application, with his part properly filled out. You must complete the application and send it to the AKC with the proper fee. Every puppy must come from a litter that has been AKC-registered by the breeder, born in the US and from a sire and dam that are also registered with the AKC.

The seller must provide you with complete records to identify the puppy. The AKC requires that the seller provide the buyer with the following: breed; sex, color and markings; date of birth; litter number (when available); names and registration numbers of the parents; breeder's name; and date sold or delivered.

FOOD AND WATER BOWLS

Your puppy will need separate bowls for his food and water. Stainless steel pans are generally preferred over plastic bowls since they sterilize better and pups are less inclined to chew on the metal. Heavy-duty ceramic bowls are popular, but consider how often you will have to pick up those heavy bowls. Buy adult-sized pans, as your puppy will grow into them quickly.

THE DOG CRATE

If you think that crates are tools of punishment and confinement for when a dog has misbehaved, think again. Most breeders and almost all trainers recommend a crate as the preferred house-training aid as well as for all-around puppy training and safety. Because dogs are natural den creatures that prefer cave-like environments, the benefits of crate use are many. The crate provides the puppy with his very

Food and water bowls should be made of sturdy, chew-resistant material, as nothing is safe from puppy teeth.

either one, so the choice is up to you. The wire crates offer better visibility for the pup as well as better ventilation. Many of the wire crates easily fold into suitcase-size carriers. The fiberglass crates, similar to those used by the airlines for animal transport, are sturdier and more den-like. However, the fiberglass crates do not fold down and are less ventilated than wire crates; this can be problematic in hot weather. Some of the newer crates are made of heavy plastic mesh; they are very lightweight and fold up into slim-line suitcases. However, a mesh crate might not be suitable for a pup with manic chewing habits.

Don't bother with a puppy-sized crate. Although your Bedlington Terrier will be a wee fellow when you bring him home, he will grow up in the blink of an eye and your puppy crate will be useless. Purchase a crate that will accommodate an adult Bedlington Terrier. A crate

The three most popular crate types: mesh on the left, wire on the right and fiberglass on top.

An open fireplace looks inviting but spells danger—the importance of puppy-proofing cannot be stressed enough!

own "safe house," a cozy place to sleep, take a break or seek comfort with a favorite safe toy; a travel aid to house your dog when on the road, at motels or at the vet's office; a training aid to help teach your puppy proper toileting habits; and a place of solitude when non-dog people happen to drop by and don't want a lively puppy—or even a well-behaved adult dog—saying hello or begging for attention.

Crates come in several types, although the wire crate and the fiberglass airline-type crate are the most popular. Both are safe and your puppy will adjust to

measuring about 30 inches long by 23 inches wide by 24 inches tall should fit him nicely.

BEDDING AND CRATE PADS

Your puppy will enjoy some type of soft bedding in his "room" (the crate), something he can snuggle into to feel cozy and secure. Old towels or blankets are good choices for a young pup, since he may (and probably will) have a toileting accident or two in the crate or decide to chew on the bedding material. Once he is fully trained and out of the early chewing stage, you can replace the puppy bedding with a perma-nent crate pad if you prefer. Crate pads and other dog beds run the gamut from inexpensive to high-end doggie-designer styles, but don't splurge on the good stuff until you are sure that your

puppy is reliable and won't tear it up or make a mess on it.

PUPPY TOYS

Just as infants and older children require objects to stimulate their minds and bodies, puppies need toys to entertain their curious brains, wiggly paws and achy teeth. A fun array of safe doggie toys will help satisfy your puppy's chewing instincts and distract him from gnawing on the leg of your antique chair or your new leather sofa. Most puppy toys are cute and look as if they would be a lot of fun, but not all are necessarily safe or good for your puppy, so use caution when you go puppy-toy shopping.

All terriers are known for their teeth! The best "chewci-fiers" are nylon and hard rubber bones that are safe to gnaw on and come in sizes appropriate for all age groups and breeds. Be especially careful of natural

Although puppies will welcome almost any toy for play, owners must be careful that the chosen playthings are safe for the curious and active Bedlington Terrier.

THE FAMILY TREE

Your puppy's pedigree is his family tree. Just as a child may resemble his parents and grandparents, so too will a puppy reflect the qualities, good and bad, of his ancestors, especially those in the first two generations. Therefore it's important to know as much as possible about a puppy's immediate relatives. Reputable and experienced breeders should be able to explain the pedigree and why they chose to breed from the particular dogs they used.

MEET THE PARENTS

Because puppies are a combination of genes inherited from both of their parents, they will reflect the qualities and temperament of their sire and dam. When visiting a litter of pups, spend time with the dam and observe her behavior with her puppies, the breeder and with strangers. The sire is often not on the premises, but the dam should be with her pups until they are eight weeks old. If either parent is surly, quarrelsome or fearful, it's likely that some of the pups will inherit those tendencies.

bones, which can splinter or develop dangerous sharp edges; pups can easily swallow or choke on those bone splinters. Veterinarians often tell of surgical nightmares involving bits of splintered bone, because in addition to the danger of choking, the sharp pieces can damage the intestinal tract.

Similarly, rawhide chews, while a favorite of most dogs and puppies, can be equally dangerous. Pieces of rawhide are easily swallowed after they get soft and gummy from chewing, and dogs have been known to choke on pieces of ingested rawhide. Rawhide chews should be offered only when you can supervise the puppy.

Soft woolly toys are special puppy favorites and can get a terrier's instincts going! They come in a wide variety of cute shapes and sizes; some look like little stuffed animals. Puppies love to shake them up and toss them about, or simply carry them around. Be careful of fuzzy toys that have button eyes or noses that your pup could chew off and swallow, and make sure that he does not disembowel a squeaky toy to remove the squeaker. Braided rope toys are similar in that they are fun to chew and toss around, but they shred easily and the strings are easy to swallow. The strings are not digestible, and if the puppy doesn't pass them in his stool, he could end up at the vet's office. As with rawhides, your puppy should be closely monitored with rope toys.

If you believe that your pup has ingested a piece of one of his toys, check his stools for the next couple of days to see if he passes the item when he defecates. At the same time, also watch for signs of intestinal distress. A call to your veterinarian might be in order to get his advice and be on the safe side.

An all-time favorite toy for puppies (young and old!) is the empty gallon milk jug. Hard plastic juice containers—46 ounces or more—are also excellent. Such containers make lots of noise when they are batted about, and puppies go crazy with delight as they play with them. However, they don't often last very long, so be sure to remove and replace them when they get chewed up.

A word of caution about homemade toys: be careful with your choices of non-traditional play objects. Never use old shoes or socks, since a puppy cannot distinguish between the old ones on which he's allowed to chew and the new ones in your closet that are strictly off limits. That principle applies to anything that resembles something that you don't want your puppy to chew.

COLLARS

A lightweight nylon collar is the best choice for a young pup. Quick-click collars are easy to put on and remove, and they can be adjusted as the puppy grows. Introduce him to his collar as soon as he comes home to get him accustomed to wearing it. He'll get used to it quickly and won't mind a bit. Make sure that

CRATE EXPECTATIONS

To make the crate more inviting to your puppy, you can offer his first meal or two inside the crate, always keeping the crate door open so that he does not feel confined. Keep a favorite safe toy or two in the crate for him to play with while inside. You can also cover the crate at night with a lightweight sheet to make it more den-like and remove the stimuli of household activity. Never put him into his crate as punishment or as you are scolding him, since he will then associate his crate with negative situations and avoid going in there.

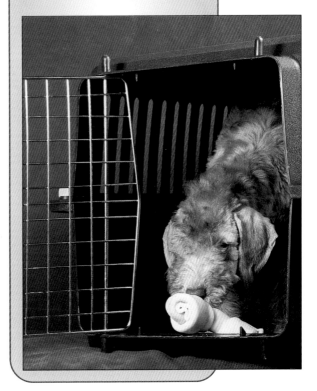

TOYS 'R SAFE

The vast array of tantalizing puppy toys is staggering. Stroll through any pet shop or pet-supply outlet and you will see that the choices can be overwhelming. However, not all dog toys are safe or sensible. Most very young puppies enjoy soft woolly toys that they can snuggle with and carry around. (You know they have outgrown them when they shred them up!) Avoid toys that have buttons, tabs or other enhancements that can be chewed off and swallowed. Soft toys that squeak are fun, but make sure your puppy does not disembowel the toy and remove (and swallow) the squeaker. Toys that rattle or make noise can excite a puppy, but they present the same danger as the squeaky kind and so require supervision. Hard rubber toys that bounce can also entertain a pup, but make sure that the toy is too big for your pup to swallow.

it is snug enough that it won't slip off, yet loose enough to be comfortable for the pup. You should be able to slip two fingers between the collar and his neck. Check the collar often, as puppies grow in spurts, and his collar can become too tight almost overnight.

LEASHES

A 6-foot nylon lead is an excellent choice for a young puppy. It is lightweight and not as tempting to chew as a leather lead. You can switch to a 6-foot leather lead after your pup has grown and is used to walking politely on a lead. For initial puppy walks and house-training purposes, you should invest in a shorter lead so that you have more control over the puppy. At first, you don't want him wandering too far away from you, and when taking him out for toileting you will want to keep him in the specific area chosen for his potty spot.

Once the puppy is heel-trained with a traditional leash, you can consider purchasing a retractable lead. A retractable lead is excellent for walking adult dogs that are already leash-wise. This type of lead allows the dog to roam farther away from you and explore a wider area when out walking, and also retracts when you need to keep him close to you.

HOME SAFETY FOR YOUR PUPPY

The importance of puppy-proofing cannot be overstated. In addition to making your house comfortable for your Bedlington Terrier's arrival, you also must make sure

The cast on this young Bedlington's leg is a testament to the trouble that puppies can get into. Provide supervision to ensure that accidents don't happen.

> ### TEETHING TIME
>
> All puppies chew. It's normal canine behavior. Chewing just plain feels good to a puppy, especially during the three- to five-month teething period when the adult teeth are breaking through the gums. Rather than attempting to eliminate such a strong natural chewing instinct, you will be more successful if you redirect it and teach your puppy what he may or may not chew. Correct inappropriate chewing with a sharp "No!" and offer him a chew toy, praising him when he takes it. Don't become discouraged. Chewing usually decreases after the adult teeth have come in.

that your house is safe for your puppy before you bring him home. There are countless hazards in the owner's personal living environment that a pup can sniff, chew, swallow or destroy. Many are obvious; others are not. Do a thorough advance house check to remove or rearrange those things that could hurt your puppy, keeping any potentially dangerous items out of areas to which he will have access.

Electrical cords are especially dangerous, since puppies view them as irresistible chew toys. Unplug and remove all exposed cords or fasten them beneath baseboards where the puppy cannot reach them. Veterinarians and firefighters can tell you horror stories about electrical burns and house

COST OF OWNERSHIP

The purchase price of your puppy is merely the first expense in the typical dog budget. Quality dog food, veterinary care (sickness and health maintenance), dog supplies and grooming costs will add up to big bucks every year. Can you adequately afford to support a canine addition to the family?

poison or other toxic chemicals in any puppy area and that you must keep such containers safely locked up. You will be amazed at how many places a curious puppy can discover!

Once your house has cleared inspection, check your yard. A sturdy fence, well embedded into the ground, will give your dog a safe place to play and potty. Bedlington Terriers are athletic dogs, so a 6-foot-high fence is necessary to contain an agile youngster or adult. Remember also that "terrier" means "earth dog," so the fence should be well embedded into the ground to prevent digging under. Check the fence periodically for necessary repairs. If there is a weak link or space to squeeze through, you can be sure a determined Bedlington will discover it.

The garage and shed can be hazardous places for a pup, as things like fertilizers, chemicals and tools are usually kept there. It's best to keep these areas off limits to the pup. Antifreeze is especially dangerous to dogs, as they find the taste appealing and it takes only a few licks from the driveway to kill a dog, puppy or adult, small breed or large.

fires that resulted from puppy-chewed electrical cords. Consider this a most serious precaution for your puppy and the rest of your family.

Scout your home for tiny objects that might be seen at a pup's eye level. Keep medication bottles and cleaning supplies well out of reach, and do the same with waste baskets and other trash containers. It goes without saying that you should not use rodent

VISITING THE VETERINARIAN

A good veterinarian is your Bedlington Terrier puppy's best health-insurance policy. If you do not already have a vet, ask friends

A Dog-Safe Home

The dog-safety police are taking you on a house tour. Let's go room by room and see how safe your own home is for your new pup. The following items are doggy dangers, so either they must be removed or the dog should be monitored or not have access to these areas.

Living Room

- house plants (some varieties are poisonous)
- fireplace or wood-burning stove
- paint on the walls (lead-based paint is toxic)
- lead drapery weights (toxic lead)
- lamps and electrical cords
- carpet cleaners or deodorizers

Outdoor

- swimming pool
- pesticides
- toxic plants
- lawn fertilizers

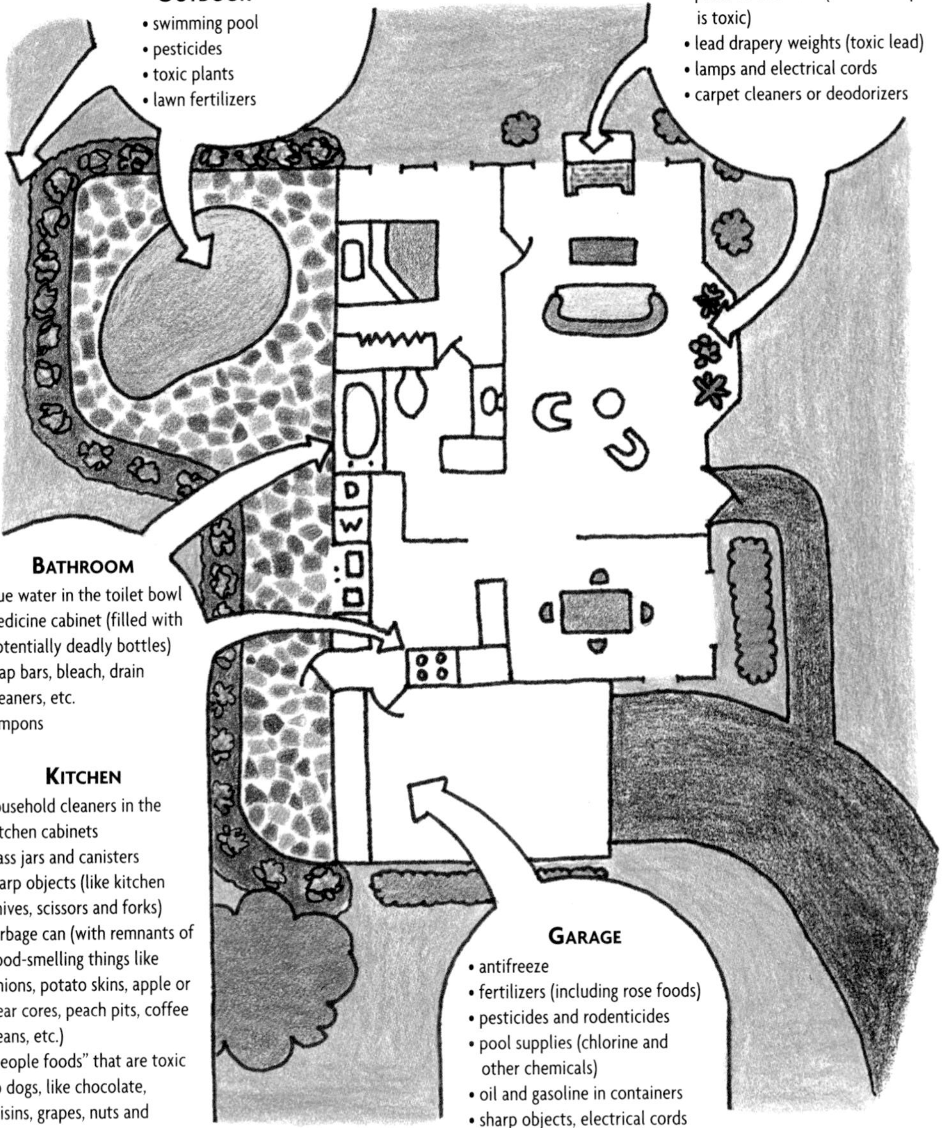

Bathroom

- blue water in the toilet bowl
- medicine cabinet (filled with potentially deadly bottles)
- soap bars, bleach, drain cleaners, etc.
- tampons

Kitchen

- household cleaners in the kitchen cabinets
- glass jars and canisters
- sharp objects (like kitchen knives, scissors and forks)
- garbage can (with remnants of good-smelling things like onions, potato skins, apple or pear cores, peach pits, coffee beans, etc.)
- "people foods" that are toxic to dogs, like chocolate, raisins, grapes, nuts and onions

Garage

- antifreeze
- fertilizers (including rose foods)
- pesticides and rodenticides
- pool supplies (chlorine and other chemicals)
- oil and gasoline in containers
- sharp objects, electrical cords and power tools

and experienced dog people in your area for recommendations so that you can select a vet before you bring your Bedlington Terrier puppy home. Also arrange for your puppy's first veterinary examination beforehand, since many vets do not have appointments immediately available and your puppy should visit the vet within a day or so of coming home.

It's important to make sure your puppy's first visit to the vet is a pleasant and positive one. The vet should take great care to befriend the pup and handle him gently to make their first meeting a positive experience. The vet will give the pup a thorough physical examination and set up a schedule for vaccinations and other necessary wellness visits. Be sure to show your vet any health and inoculation records, which you should have received from your breeder. Your vet is a great source of canine health information, so be sure to ask questions and take notes. Creating a health journal for your puppy will make a handy reference for his wellness and any future health problems that may arise.

MEETING THE FAMILY
Your Bedlington Terrier's homecoming is an exciting time for all members of the family, and it's only natural that everyone will be eager to meet him, pet him and play with him. However, for the puppy's sake,

it's best to make these initial family meetings as uneventful as possible so that the pup is not overwhelmed with too much too soon. Remember, he has just left his dam and his littermates and is away from the breeder's home for the first time. Despite his wagging tail, he is still apprehensive and wondering where he is and who all these strange humans are. It's best to let him explore on his own and meet the family members as he feels comfortable. Let him investigate all the new smells, sights and sounds at his own pace. Children should be especially careful to not get overly excited, use loud voices or hug the pup too tightly. Be calm, gentle and affectionate, and be ready to comfort him if he appears frightened or uneasy.

Be sure to show your puppy his new crate during this first day home. Toss a treat or two inside the crate; if he associates the crate with food, he will associate the crate with good things. If he is comfortable with the crate, you can offer him his first meal inside it. Leave the door ajar so he can wander in and out as he chooses.

FIRST NIGHT IN HIS NEW HOME
So much has happened in your Bedlington Terrier puppy's first day away from the breeder. He's

had his first car ride to his new home. He's met his new human family and perhaps the other family pets. He has explored his new house and yard, at least those places where he is to be allowed during his first weeks at home. He may have visited his new veterinarian. He has eaten his first meal or two away from his dam and littermates. Surely that's enough to tire out an eight-week-old Bedlington Terrier pup—or so you hope!

It's bedtime. During the day, the pup investigated his crate, which is his new den and sleeping space, so it is not entirely strange to him. Line the crate with a soft towel or blanket that he can snuggle into and gently place him into the crate for the night. Some breeders send home a piece of bedding from where the pup slept with his littermates, and those familiar scents are a great comfort for the puppy on his first night without his siblings.

He will probably whine or cry. The puppy is objecting to the confinement and the fact that he is alone for the first time. This can be a stressful time for you as well as for the pup. It's important that you remain strong and don't let the puppy out of his crate to comfort him. He will fall asleep eventually. If you release him, the puppy will learn that crying means "out" and will continue

that habit. You are laying the groundwork for future habits. Some breeders find that soft music can soothe a crying pup and help him get to sleep.

SOCIALIZING YOUR PUPPY

The first 20 weeks of your Bedlington Terrier puppy's life are the most important of his entire lifetime. A properly socialized puppy will grow up to be a confident and stable adult who will be a pleasure to live with and a welcome addition to the neighborhood.

The importance of socialization cannot be overemphasized.

"Are you my mommy?" baby Mouse asks her young friend.

Puppies learn canine behavior from their siblings. These two Bedlington pups will teach each other a thing or two before they head to their new homes.

especially children. Puppies automatically recognize children as "little people" and are drawn to play with them. Just make sure that you supervise these meetings and that the children do not get too rough or encourage him to play too hard. An overzealous pup can often nip too hard, frightening the child and in turn making the puppy overly excited. A bad experience in puppyhood can impact a dog for life, so a pup that has a negative experience with a child may grow up to be shy or even aggressive around children.

Research on canine behavior has proven that puppies who are not exposed to new sights, sounds, people and animals during their first 20 weeks of life will grow up to be timid and fearful, even aggressive, and unable to flourish outside of their familiar home environment.

Socializing your puppy is not difficult and, in fact, will be a fun time for you both. Lead training goes hand in hand with socialization, so your puppy will be learning how to walk on a lead at the same time that he's meeting the neighborhood. Because the Bedlington Terrier is such a unique and remarkable breed, everyone will enjoy meeting "the new kid on the block." Take him for short walks, to the park and to other dog-friendly places where he will encounter new people,

Take your puppy along on your daily errands. Puppies are natural "people magnets," and most people who see your pup will want to pet him. All of these

MEET AND MINGLE

Puppies need to meet people and see the world if they are to grow up confident and unafraid. Take your puppy with you on everyday outings and errands. On-lead walks around the neighborhood and to the park offer the pup good exposure to the goings-on of his new human world. Avoid areas frequented by other dogs until your puppy has had his full round of puppy shots; ask your vet when your pup will be properly protected. Arrange for your puppy to meet new people of all ages every week.

encounters will help to mold him into a confident adult dog. Likewise, you will soon feel like a confident, responsible dog owner, rightly proud of your mannerly Bedlington Terrier.

Be especially careful of your puppy's encounters and experiences during the eight- to ten-week-old period, which is also called the "fear period." This is a serious imprinting period, and all contact during this time should be gentle and positive. A frightening or negative event could leave a permanent impression that could affect his future behavior if a similar situation arises.

Also make sure that your puppy has received his first and second rounds of vaccinations before you expose him to other dogs or bring him to places that other dogs may frequent. Avoid dog parks and other strange-dog areas until your vet assures you that your puppy is fully immunized and resistant to the diseases that can be passed between canines. Discuss socialization with your breeder, as some breeders recommend socializing the puppy even before he has received all of his inoculations, depending on how outgoing the puppy may be.

LEADER OF THE PUPPY'S PACK

Like other canines, your puppy needs an authority figure, someone he can look up to and regard as the leader of his "pack." His first pack leader was his dam, who taught him to be polite and not chew too hard on her ears or nip at her muzzle. He learned those same lessons from his littermates. If he played too

TOXIC PLANTS

Plants are natural puppy magnets, but many can be harmful, even fatal, if ingested by a puppy or adult dog. Scout your yard and home interior and remove any plants, bushes or flowers that could be even mildly dangerous. It could save your puppy's life. You can obtain a complete list of toxic plants from your veterinarian, at the public library or by looking online.

rough, they cried in pain and stopped the game, which sent an important message to the rowdy puppy.

As puppies play together, they are also struggling to determine who will be the boss. Being pack animals, dogs need someone to be in charge. If a litter of puppies remained together beyond puppyhood, one of the pups would emerge as the strongest one, the one who calls the shots.

Once your puppy leaves the pack, he will look intuitively for a new leader. If he does not recognize you as that leader, he will try to assume that position for himself. Of course, it is hard to imagine your adorable Bedlington Terrier puppy trying to be in charge when he is so small and

Give your Bedlington pup time to adjust to his new home. Do not overwhelm him, but give him encouragement, praise and things to make him comfortable as he settles in.

seemingly helpless. You must remember that these are natural canine instincts. Do not cave in and allow your pup to get the upper "paw"!

Just as socialization is so important during these first 20 weeks, so too is your puppy's early education. He was born without any bad habits. He does not know what is good or bad behavior. If he does things like nipping and digging, it's because he is having fun and doesn't know that humans consider these things as "bad." It's your job to teach him proper puppy manners, and this is the best time to accomplish that, before he has developed bad habits, since it is much more diffi-cult to "unlearn" or correct unac-ceptable learned behavior than to teach good behavior from the start.

Make sure that all members of the family understand the impor-tance of being consistent when training their new puppy. If you tell the puppy to stay off the sofa and your daughter allows him to cuddle on the couch to watch her favorite television show, your pup will be confused about what he is and is not allowed to do. Have a family conference before your pup comes home so that everyone understands the basic principles of puppy training and the rules you have set forth for the pup and agrees to follow them.

The old saying that "an ounce of prevention is worth a pound of

SWEETS THAT KILL
Antifreeze would be every dog's favorite topping for a chocolate sundae! However, antifreeze, just like chocolate, kills dogs. Ethylene glycol, found in antifreeze, causes acute renal failure in dogs and can be fatal. Dogs suffering from kidney failure expel little or no urine, act lethargically, may experience vomiting or diarrhea and may resist activity and drinking water. Just a single teaspoon of antifreeze is enough to kill a dog (depending on the size); even for large dogs it takes only a tablespoon or two! Like that chocolate ice cream, antifreeze is sweet-tasting and smells yummy. Keep both away from your dog!

cure" is especially true when it comes to puppies. It is much easier to prevent inappropriate behavior than it is to change it. It's also easier and less stressful for the pup, since it will keep discipline to a minimum and create a more positive learning environment for him. That, in turn, will also be easier on you.

Here are a few commonsense tips to keep your belongings safe and your puppy out of trouble:
• Keep your closet doors closed and your shoes, socks and other apparel off the floor so your puppy can't get to them.
• Keep a secure lid on the trash container or put the trash where

SOLVING PUPPY PROBLEMS

CHEWING AND NIPPING

Nipping at fingers and toes is normal puppy behavior. Chewing is also the way that puppies investigate their surroundings. However, you will have to teach your puppy that chewing anything other than his toys is not acceptable. That won't happen overnight and at times puppy teeth will test your patience. However, if you allow nipping and chewing to continue, just think about the damage that a mature Bedlington Terrier can do with a full set of adult terrier teeth.

Whenever your puppy nips your hand or fingers, cry out "Ouch!" in a loud voice, which

A Bedlington Terrier that is properly socialized as a pup will grow up into a friendly dog that is eager to make new acquaintances.

your puppy can't dig into it. He can't damage what he can't reach!

- Supervise your puppy at all times to make sure he is not getting into mischief. If he starts to chew the corner of the rug, you can distract him instantly by tossing a toy for him to fetch. You also will be able to whisk him outside when you notice that he is about to piddle on the carpet. If you can't see your puppy, you can't teach him or correct his behavior.

DIGGING OUT

Some dogs love to dig, and terriers are certainly talented excavators. Digging is considered "self-rewarding behavior" because it's fun! Of all the digging solutions offered by the experts, most are only marginally successful and none are guaranteed to work. The best cure is prevention, which means removing the dog from the offending site when he digs as well as distracting him when you catch him digging so that he turns his attentions elsewhere. That means that you have to supervise your dog's yard time. An unsupervised digger can create havoc with your landscaping or, worse, run away!

GETTING ACQUAINTED
When visiting a litter, ask the breeder for suggestions on how best to interact with the puppies. If possible, get right into the middle of the pack and sit down with them. Observe which pups climb into your lap and which ones shy away. Toss a toy for them to chase and bring back to you. It's easy to fall in love with the puppy who picks you, but keep your future objectives in mind before you make your final decision.

should startle your puppy and stop him from nipping, even if only for a moment. Immediately distract him by offering a small treat or an appropriate toy for him to chew instead (which means having chew toys and puppy treats handy or in your pockets at all times). Praise him when he takes the toy and tell him what a good fellow he is. Praise is just as or even more important in puppy training as discipline and correction.

Puppies also tend to nip at children more often than adults, since they perceive little ones to be more vulnerable and more similar to their littermates. Teach your children appropriate responses to nipping behavior. If they are unable to handle it themselves, you may have to intervene. Puppy nips can be quite painful,

and a child's frightened reaction will only encourage a puppy to nip harder, which is a natural canine response. As with all other puppy situations, interaction between your Bedlington Terrier puppy and children should be supervised.

Chewing on objects, not just family members' fingers and ankles, is also normal canine behavior that can be especially tedious (for the owner, not the pup) during the teething period when the puppy's adult teeth are coming in. At this stage, chewing just plain feels good. Furniture legs and cabinet corners are common puppy favorites. Shoes and other personal items also taste pretty good to a pup.

The best solution is, once again, prevention. If you value something, keep it tucked away and out of reach. You can't hide your dining-room table in a closet, but you can try to deflect the chewing by applying a bitter prod-

Good breeders give their Bedlington babies the best start in life. These littermates are the future Ch. Capstone One Under Par and Ch. Capstone One Over Par.

You may lose a treasure or two during your puppy's growing-up period, and the furniture could sustain a nasty nick or two. These can be trying times, so be prepared for those inevitable accidents and comfort yourself in knowing that this too shall pass.

JUMPING UP

Puppies will be puppies, and puppies jump up...on you, your guests, your counters and your furniture. Just another normal part of growing up, and one you need to meet head-on before it becomes an ingrained habit.

The key to jump correction is consistency. You cannot correct your Bedlington Terrier for jumping up on you today, then allow it to happen tomorrow by greeting him with hugs and kisses. As you have learned by now, consistency is critical to all puppy lessons.

For starters, try turning your back as soon as the puppy jumps. Jumping up is a means of gaining your attention and, if the pup can't see your face, he may get discouraged and learn that he loses eye contact with his beloved master when he jumps up.

Leash corrections also work, and most puppies respond well to a leash tug if they jump. Grasp the leash close to the puppy's collar and give a quick tug downward, using the command "Off."

Decide on the house rules and enforce them early on. If you do not want your Bedlington to share your favorite chair as an adult, don't allow him to do so as a puppy.

uct made just to deter dogs from chewing. This spray-on substance is vile-tasting, although safe for dogs, and most puppies will avoid the forbidden object after one tiny taste. You also can apply the product to your leather leash if the puppy tries to chew on his lead during leash-training sessions.

Keep a ready supply of safe chews handy to offer your Bedlington Terrier as a distraction when he starts to chew on something that's a "no-no." Remember, at this tender age he does not yet know what is permitted or forbidden, so you have to be "on call" every minute he's awake and on the prowl.

Do not use the word "Down," since "Down" is used to teach the puppy to lie down, which is a separate action that he will learn during his education in the basic commands. As soon as the puppy has backed off, tell him to sit and immediately praise him for doing so. This will take many repetitions and won't be accomplished quickly, so don't get discouraged or give up; you must be even more persistent than your puppy.

A second method used for jump correction is the spritzer bottle. Fill a spray bottle with water mixed with a bit of lemon juice or vinegar. As soon as the puppy jumps, command him "Off" and spritz him with the water mixture. Of course, that means having the spray bottle handy whenever or wherever jumping usually happens.

Yet a third method to discourage jumping is grasping the puppy's paws and holding them gently but firmly until he struggles to get away. Wait a brief moment or two, then release his paws and give him a command to sit. He should eventually learn that jumping gets him into an uncomfortable predicament.

Children are major victims of puppy jumping, since puppies view little people as ready targets for jumping up as well as nipping. If your children (or their friends) are unable to dispense jump corrections, you will have to intervene and handle it for them.

Important to prevention is also knowing what you should not do. Never kick your Bedlington (for any reason, not just for jumping) or knock him in

A SMILE'S WORTH A MILE

Don't embark on your Bedlington's training course when you're not in the mood. Never train your dog if you're feeling grouchy or impatient with him. Subjecting your dog to your bad mood is a bad move. He will sense your negative attitude, and neither of you will enjoy the session or have any measure of success. Always begin and end your training sessions on a happy note.

the chest with your knee. That maneuver could actually harm your puppy. Vets can tell you stories about puppies who suffered broken bones after being banged about when they jumped up.

PUPPY WHINING

Puppies often cry and whine, just as infants and little children do. It's their way of telling us that they are lonely or in need of attention. Your puppy will miss his littermates and will feel insecure when he is left alone. You may be out of the house or just in another room, but he will still feel alone. During these times, the puppy's crate should be his personal comfort station, a place all his own where he can feel safe and secure. Once he learns that being alone is okay and not something to be feared, he will settle down without crying or objecting. You might want to leave a radio on while he is crated, as the sound of human voices can be soothing and will give the impression that people are around.

Give your puppy a favorite cuddly toy or chew toy to entertain him whenever he is crated. You will both be happier: the puppy because he is safe in his den and you because he is quiet, safe and not getting into puppy escapades that can wreak havoc in your house or cause him danger.

To make sure that your puppy will always view his crate as a safe and cozy place, never, *ever* use the crate as punishment. That's the best way to turn the crate into a negative place that the pup will want to avoid. Sure, you can use the crate for your own peace of mind if your puppy is getting into trouble and needs some "time out." Just don't let him know that! Never scold the pup and immediately place him into the crate. Count to ten, give him a couple of hugs and maybe a treat, then scoot him into his crate.

It's also important not to make a big fuss when he is released from the crate. That will make getting out of the crate more appealing than being in the crate, which is just the opposite of what you are trying to achieve.

> **BE CONSISTENT**
>
> Consistency is a key element, in fact is absolutely necessary, to a puppy's learning environment. A behavior (such as chewing, jumping up or climbing onto the furniture) cannot be forbidden one day and then allowed the next. That will only confuse the pup, and he will not understand what he is supposed to do. Just one or two episodes of allowing an undesirable behavior to "slide" will imprint that behavior on a puppy's brain and make that behavior more difficult to erase or change.

PROPER CARE OF YOUR
BEDLINGTON TERRIER

Adding a Bedlington Terrier to your household means adding a new family member who will need your care each and every day. When your Bedlington Terrier pup first comes home, you will start a routine with him so that, as he grows up, your dog will have a daily schedule just as you do. The aspects of your dog's daily care will likewise become regular parts of your day, so you'll both have a new schedule. Dogs learn by consistency and thrive on routine: regular times for meals, exercise, grooming and potty trips are just as important for your dog as they are for you. Your dog's schedule will depend much on your family's daily routine, but remember that you now have a new member of the family who is part of your day every day!

FEEDING

Feeding your dog the best diet is based on various factors, including age, activity level, overall condition and size of the breed. When you visit the breeder, he will share with you his advice about the proper diet for your dog based on his experience with the breed and the foods with which

he has had success. Likewise, your vet will be a helpful source of advice throughout the dog's life and will aid you in planning a diet for optimal health.

FEEDING THE PUPPY

Of course, your pup's very first food will be his dam's milk. There may be special situations in which pups fail to nurse, necessitating that the breeder hand-feed them with a formula, but for the most part pups spend the first weeks of life nursing from their dam. The breeder weans the pups by gradually introducing solid foods and decreasing the milk

Discuss the puppy's feeding schedule and type of food with the breeder to learn how best to continue feeding the pup at home.

Quality dog foods are more costly than generic brands, but the nutritional value is well worth the added expense.

meals. Pups may even start themselves off on the weaning process, albeit inadvertently, if they snatch bites from their mom's food bowl.

By the time the pups are ready for new homes, they are fully weaned and eating a good puppy food. As a new owner, you may be thinking, "Great! The breeder has taken care of the hard part." Not so fast.

A puppy's first year of life is the time when all or most of his growth and development takes place. This is a delicate time, and diet plays a huge role in proper skeletal and muscular formation. Improper diet and exercise habits can lead to damaging problems that will compromise the dog's health and movement for his entire life. That being said, new

owners should not worry needlessly. With the myriad types of food formulated specifically for growing pups of different-sized breeds, dog-food manufacturers have taken much of the guesswork out of feeding your puppy well. Since growth-food formulas are designed to provide the nutrition that a growing puppy needs, it is unnecessary and, in fact, can prove harmful to add supplements to the diet. Research has shown that too much of certain vitamin supplements and minerals predispose a dog to skeletal problems. It's by no means a case of "if a little is good, a lot is better." At every stage of your dog's life, too much or too little in the way of nutrients can be harmful, which is why a manufactured complete

JUST ADD MEAT

An organic alternative to the traditional dog kibble or canned food comes in the form of grain-based feeds. These dry cereal-type products consist of oat and rye flakes, corn meal, wheat germ, dried kelp and other natural ingredients. The manufacturers recommend that the food be mixed with meat in a ratio of two parts grain to one part meat. As an alternative to fresh meat, investigate freeze-dried meat and fermented meat products, which makers claim are more nutritious and digestible for dogs.

food is the easiest way to know that your dog is getting what he needs.

Because of a young pup's small body and accordingly small digestive system, his daily portion will be divided up into small meals throughout the day. This can mean starting off with three or more meals a day and decreasing the number of meals as the pup matures. For the adult, dividing the day's food into two meals on a morning/evening schedule is healthier for the dog's digestion than one large daily portion.

Regarding the feeding schedule, feeding the pup at the same times and in the same place each day is important for both housebreaking purposes and establishing the dog's everyday routine. As for the amount to feed, growing puppies generally need proportionately more food per body weight than their adult counterparts, but a pup should never be allowed to gain excess weight. Dogs of all ages should be kept in proper body condition, but extra weight can strain a pup's developing frame, causing skeletal problems.

Watch your pup's weight as he grows and, if the recommended amounts seem to be too much or too little for your pup, consult the vet about appropriate dietary changes. Keep in mind that treats, although small, can quickly add up throughout the day, contribut-

DIET DON'TS
- Got milk? Don't give it to your dog! Dogs cannot tolerate large quantities of cows' milk, as they do not have the enzymes to digest lactose.
- You may have heard of dog owners who add raw eggs to their dogs' food for a shiny coat or to make the food more palatable, but consumption of raw eggs too often can cause a deficiency of the vitamin biotin.
- Avoid feeding table scraps, as they will upset the balance of the dog's complete food. Additionally, fatty or highly seasoned foods can cause upset canine stomachs.
- Do not offer raw meat to your dog. Raw meat can contain parasites; it also is high in fat.
- Vitamin A toxicity in dogs can be caused by too much raw liver, especially if the dog already gets enough vitamin A in his balanced diet, which should be the case.
- Bones like chicken, pork chop and other soft bones are not suitable, as they easily splinter.

ing unnecessary calories. Treats are fine when used prudently; opt for dog treats specially formulated to be healthy or for nutritious snacks like small pieces of cheese or cooked chicken.

FEEDING THE ADULT DOG

For the adult (meaning physically mature) dog, feeding properly is about maintenance, not growth. Again, correct weight is a concern. Your dog should appear fit and should have an evident "waist." His ribs should not be protruding (a sign of being underweight), but they should be covered by only a slight layer of fat. Under normal circumstances, an adult dog can be maintained fairly easily with a high-quality nutritionally complete adult-formula food.

Factor treats into your dog's overall daily caloric intake, and avoid offering table scraps. Overweight dogs are more prone to health problems. Research has even shown that obesity takes years off a dog's life. With that in mind, resist the urge to overfeed and over-treat. Don't make unnecessary additions to your dog's diet, whether with tidbits or with extra vitamins and minerals.

The amount of food needed for proper maintenance will vary depending on the individual dog's activity level, but you will be able to tell whether the daily portions are keeping him in good shape. With the wide variety of good complete foods available, choosing what to feed is largely a matter of personal preference. Just as with the puppy, the adult dog should have consistency in his mealtimes and feeding place. In addition to a consistent routine, regular mealtimes also allow the owner to see how much his dog is eating. If the dog seems never to be satisfied or, likewise, becomes uninterested in his food, the

FREE FEEDING

Many owners opt to feed their dogs the free way. That is, they serve dry kibble in a feeder or bowl that is available to the dog all day. Arguably, this is the most convenient method of feeding an adult dog, but it may encourage the dog to become fussy about food or defensive over his bowl. Free feeding is an option only for adult dogs, not puppies.

owner will know right away that something is wrong and can consult the vet.

DIETS FOR THE AGING DOG

A good rule of thumb is that once a dog has reached 75% of his expected lifespan, he has reached "senior citizen" or geriatric status. Your Bedlington Terrier will be considered a senior at about 9 years of age; based on size and breed-specific factors, he has a projected lifespan of about 12–14 years. (The smallest breeds generally enjoy the longest lives and the largest breeds the shortest.)

What does aging have to do with your dog's diet? No, he won't get a discount at the local diner's early-bird special. Yes, he will require some dietary changes to accommodate the changes that come along with increased age. One change is that the older dog's dietary needs become more similar to that of a puppy. Specifically, dogs can metabolize more protein as youngsters and seniors than in the adult-maintenance stage. Discuss with your vet at what age you need to switch to a higher-protein or senior-formulated food or whether your current adult-dog food contains sufficient nutrition for the senior.

Watching the dog's weight remains essential, even more so in the senior stage. Older dogs are already more vulnerable to illness, and obesity only

contributes to their susceptibility to problems. As the older dog becomes less active and thus exercises less, his regular portions may cause him to gain weight. At this point, you may consider decreasing his daily food intake or switching to a reduced-calorie food. As with other changes, you should consult your vet for advice.

SWITCHING FOODS

There are certain times in a dog's life when it becomes necessary to switch his food; for example, from puppy to adult food and then from adult to senior-dog food. Additionally, you may decide to feed your pup a different type of food from what he received from the breeder, and there may be "emergency" situations in which you can't find your dog's normal brand and have to offer something else temporarily. Anytime a change is made, for whatever reason, the switch must be done gradually. You don't want to upset the dog's stomach or end up with a picky eater who refuses to eat something new. A tried-and-true approach is, over the course of about a week, to mix a little of the new food in with the old, increasing the proportion of new to old as the days progress. At the end of the week, you'll be feeding his regular portions of the new food, and he will barely notice the change.

Bedlington siblings enjoy a "family-style" dinner.

DON'T FORGET THE WATER!

For a dog, it's always time for a drink. Regardless of what type of food he eats, there's no doubt that he needs plenty of water. Fresh cold water, in a clean bowl, should be freely available to your dog at all times. There are special circumstances, such as during puppy housebreaking, when you will want to monitor your pup's water intake so that you will be able to predict when he will need to relieve himself, but water must be available to him nonetheless. Water is essential for hydration and proper body function just as it is for humans.

You will get to know how much your dog typically drinks in a day. Of course, in the heat or if exercising vigorously, he will be more thirsty and will drink more. However, if he begins to drink noticeably more water for no apparent reason, this could signal any of various problems, and you are advised to consult your vet.

Water is the best drink for dogs. Some owners are tempted to give milk from time to time or to moisten dry food with milk, but dogs do not have the enzymes necessary to digest the lactose in milk, which is much different from the milk that nursing puppies receive. Therefore stick with clean fresh water to quench your dog's thirst, and always have it readily available to him.

EXERCISE

The terrier breeds are active dogs that require considerable exercise to stay fit and mentally balanced. Regardless of breed, a sedentary lifestyle is as harmful to a dog as it

---

NOT HUNGRY?

No dog in his right mind would turn down his dinner, would he? If you notice that your dog has lost interest in his food, there could be any number of causes. Dental problems are a common cause of appetite loss, one that is often overlooked. If your dog has a toothache, a loose tooth or sore gums from infection, chances are it doesn't feel so good to chew. Think about when you've had a toothache! If your dog does not approach the food bowl with his usual enthusiasm, look inside his mouth for signs of a problem. Whatever the cause, you'll want to consult your vet so that your chow hound can get back to his happy, hungry self as soon as possible.

is to a person, and, with the Bedlington Terrier, more is more when it comes to activity. Nonetheless, you don't have to be an Olympic athlete to provide your dog with a sufficient amount of exercise. Fortunately, those Bedlington limbs are short and you don't have to run 5 miles a day to keep your buddy fit. Exercising your Bedlington Terrier can be enjoyable and healthy for both of you. Brisk walks, once the puppy reaches three or four months of age, will stimulate heart rates and build muscle for both dog and owner. As the dog reaches adulthood, the speed and distance of the walks can be increased as long as they are both kept reasonable and comfortable for both of you.

Play sessions in the yard and letting the dog run free in the yard under your supervision also are sufficient forms of exercise for the Bedlington Terrier. Fetching games can be played indoors or out; these are excellent for giving your dog active play that he will enjoy. Chasing things that move comes naturally to dogs of all breeds, and the Bedlington is the king of the chase. If you choose to play games outdoors, you must have a securely fenced-in yard and/or have the dog attached to at least a 25-foot light line for security. You want your Bedlington Terrier to run, but not run away!

Bear in mind that an overweight dog should never be suddenly over-exercised; instead he should be encouraged to increase exercise slowly. Not only is exercise essential to keep the dog's body fit, it is essential to his mental well-being. A bored dog will find something to do, which often manifests itself in some type

QUENCHING HIS THIRST

Is your dog drinking more than normal and trying to lap up everything in sight? Excessive drinking has many different causes. Obvious causes for a dog's being thirstier than usual are hot weather and vigorous exercise. However, if your dog is drinking more for no apparent reason, you could have cause for concern. Serious conditions like kidney or liver disease, diabetes and various types of hormonal problems can all be indicated by excessive drinking. If you notice your dog's being excessively thirsty, contact your vet at once. Hopefully there will be a simpler explanation, but the earlier a serious problem is detected, the sooner it can be treated, with a better rate of cure.

of destructive behavior. In this sense, exercise is essential for the owner's mental well-being as well!

GROOMING

Most dogs, no matter how short the coat, will require some grooming so that you can have a dog that can live in the house with you, who will be a reputable family member, who is clean and who smells nice. Do be aware when considering a Bedlington Terrier as a pet that this is a breed that needs grooming. If the dog is not groomed, you will eventually have a matted dog who will no longer resemble the lamb-like look that appealed to you when you purchased your Bedlington. The plus side of a Bedlington is that, unlike most other breeds, he is a non-shedding dog. However, he

does need grooming to eliminate the dead hair, as this is what will mat if not removed.

If you are purchasing your Bedlington as a show dog, he will need extensive grooming. This is a skill that is best learned from an experienced individual such as the breeder of your pup. This is also a skill that cannot be learned in an hour or even a day, as it takes time and experience to perfect the well-groomed dog for the show ring.

Since the vast majority of dog owners buy their dogs for companions rather than show dogs, we will assume that you will be doing a pet clip for your dog. This is perfectly acceptable and relatively easy to do, and you will have a dog that looks like the proper Bedlington.

There is some basic equipment that you will need before starting. You will need a grooming table, which is a sturdy table with a non-skid surface covering the top. On this you will have an arm, or "hanger," with which you will attach the leash so that your dog cannot jump off the table or lie down "on the job," as this makes grooming extremely difficult. Stop by your local pet-supply store and they will show you what you will need.

You will also need a steel comb, a slicker brush, a sharp pair of barber scissors and a toenail trimmer. Be sure that your scissors

---

PUPPY STEPS

Puppies are brimming with activity and enthusiasm. It seems that they can play all day and night without tiring, but don't overdo your puppy's exercise regimen. Easy does it for the puppy's first six to nine months. Keep walks brief and don't let the puppy engage in stressful jumping games. The puppy frame is delicate, and too much exercise during those critical growing months can cause injury to his bone structure, ligaments and musculature. Save his first jog for his first birthday!

are sharp, as a dull pair will be difficult to use and will not do a neat job. You will also need electric clippers with a #15 (or #30 or #40) blade for close work and a #5 blade for clipping the body.

The Bedlington Terrier Club of America offers show- and pet-grooming diagrams and advice on its website (www.bedlingtonamerica.com). Here also is a method of doing a pet trim:

Put your dog on the grooming table and thoroughly comb out the entire dog. Look at a picture of a groomed Bedlington and try to envision your dog in the proper clip.

After your dog is combed out, pick up your clipper and, with the finer (#15) blade, clip the dog's ears, leaving a little tuft at the bottom of the ears. Then, clip the face, throat, tuck-up, belly and tail. (*Note:* Cutting against the direction of the hair growth gives a more even and shorter trim.)

Next, with your #5 blade, clip the back of the hind legs, stopping about 3 inches above the hock joint where the leg begins to get thicker. Continue with the #5 blade and clip the front edge of the thighs, the tail root, the whole back, but not the brisket, to below the widest part of the ribs.

Continue to clip the chest and shoulders down to the elbows. The throat and sides of the neck will be trimmed to below the base of the ears, but leave a strip like a

horse's mane down the back of the neck. Comb out the hair on the legs, brisket, head and neck; with your scissors, cut the long hair so that it blends into the clipped areas. Cut the hair shorter on the back of the neck, the elbows and the sides of the body. Trim the hair on the feet and legs, and, of course, trim the toenails with your toenail clipper.

Remember, this will be a bit tricky the first few times you do

SCOOTING HIS BOTTOM

Here's a doggy problem that many owners tend to neglect. If your dog is scooting his rear end around the carpet, he probably is experiencing anal-sac impaction or blockage. The anal sacs are the two grape-sized glands on either side of the dog's vent. The dog cannot empty these glands, which become filled with a foul-smelling material. The dog may attempt to lick the area to relieve the pressure. He may also rub his anus on your walls, furniture or floors.

Don't neglect your dog's rear end during grooming sessions. By squeezing both sides of the anus with a soft cloth, you can express some of the material in the sacs. If the material is pasty and thick, you likely will need the assistance of a veterinarian. Vets know how to express the glands and can show you how to do it correctly without hurting the dog or spraying yourself with the unpleasant liquid.

The ear before clipping and trimming.

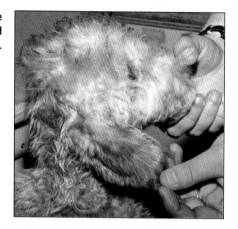

Cutting around the edge of the ear.

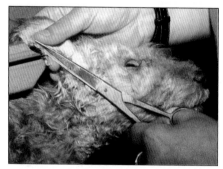

The finished ear.

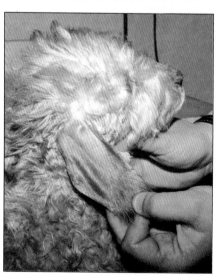

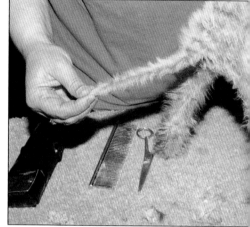

Puppy tail prior to grooming.

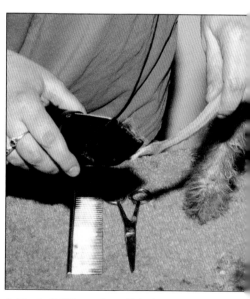

Putting the finishing touches to the tail.

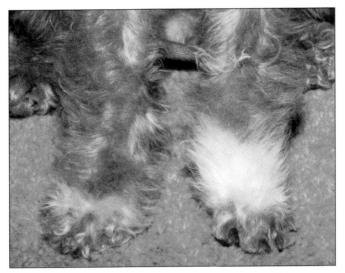

A puppy with the left leg untrimmed and the right leg trimmed.

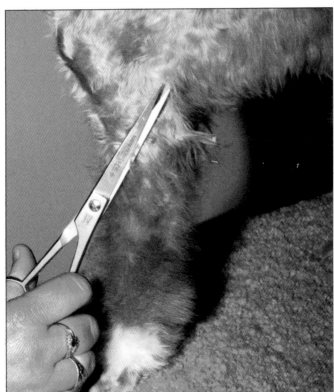

Scissors are used to neaten up the legs.

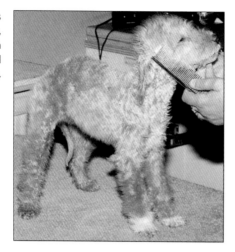

The facial hair is combed gently, using a comb with widely spaced teeth.

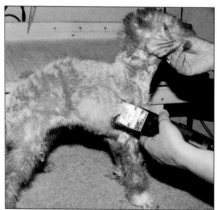

Trimming the puppy coat with electric clippers.

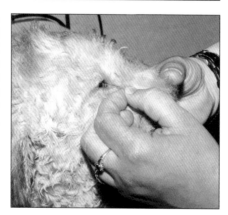

Use a specially formulated cleaner and cotton wipe around the eyes to clean the area and remove any tear stains.

it, but with each grooming you will become more experienced. I grew up with a Wire Fox Terrier, which my mother learned to groom by herself. The dog always looked like a proper Wire Fox Terrier even though she was never trimmed to the extent that a show dog would be. After a few experiences of grooming, you and your dog will walk down the street and passers-by will say, "Look, that dog looks like a lamb!"

You should comb out your dog's coat once a week and give a bath as needed. Your dog will probably need a trimming about every three months and, if you keep up with your grooming, once you have set the grooming pattern you will find that the next grooming will be much easier. Of course, you can always take your dog to a grooming shop to be cleaned up, usually every three months, but you may enjoy the challenge of learning to groom, and it gives you some quality time with your pet.

BATHING

In general, dogs need to be bathed only a few times a year, possibly more often if your dog gets into something messy or if he starts to smell like a dog. Show dogs are usually bathed more frequently, depending on the show schedule and the owner. Bathing too frequently can have negative effects on the skin and coat, removing natural oils and causing dryness.

If you give your dog his first bath when he is young, he will become accustomed to the process. Wrestling a dog into the tub or chasing a freshly shampooed dog who has escaped from the bath will be no fun! Most dogs don't naturally enjoy their baths, but you at least want yours to cooperate with you.

Before bathing the dog, have the items you'll need close at hand. First, decide where you will bathe the dog. You should have a tub or basin with a non-slip surface. Puppies can even be bathed in a sink. In warm weather, some like to use a portable pool in the yard, although you'll want to make sure your dog doesn't head for the nearest dirt pile following his bath! You will also need a hose or shower spray to wet the coat thoroughly, a shampoo formulated for dogs, absorbent towels and perhaps a blow dryer. Human shampoos are too harsh for dogs' coats and will dry them out.

Before wetting the dog, give him a brush-through to remove any dead hair, dirt and mats. Make sure he is at ease in the tub and have the water at a comfortable temperature. Begin bathing by wetting the coat all the way down to the skin. Massage in the shampoo, keeping it away from his face and eyes. Rinse him thoroughly,

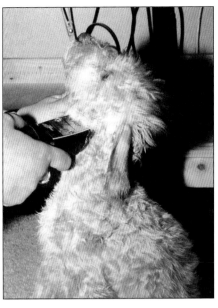

The throat area should be closely trimmed.

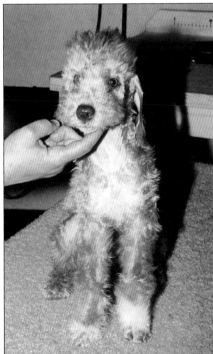

The throat after trimming.

again avoiding the eyes and ears, as you don't want to get water into the ear canals. A thorough rinsing is important, as shampoo residue is drying and itchy to the dog. After rinsing, wrap him in a towel to absorb the initial moisture. You can finish drying with either a towel or a blow dryer on low heat, held at a safe distance from the dog. You should keep the dog indoors and away from drafts until he is completely dry.

NAIL CLIPPING

Having their nails trimmed is not on many dogs' lists of favorite things to do. With this in mind, you will need to accustom your puppy to the procedure at a young age so that he will sit still (well, as still as he can) for his pedicures. Long nails can cause the dog's feet to spread, which is not good for him; likewise, long nails can hurt if they unintentionally scratch, not good for you!

Some dogs' nails are worn down naturally by regular walking on hard surfaces, so the frequency with which you clip depends on your individual dog. Look at his nails from time to time and clip as needed; a good way to know when it's time for a trim is if you hear your dog clicking as he walks across the floor.

There are several types of nail clippers and even electric nail-grinding tools made for dogs. First we'll discuss using the clip-

per. To start, have your clipper ready and some doggie treats on hand. You want your pup to view his nail-clipping sessions in a positive light, and what better way to convince him than with food? You may want to enlist the help of an assistant to comfort the pup and offer treats as you concentrate on the clipping itself. The guillotine-type clipper is thought of by many as the easiest type to use; the nail tip is inserted into the opening, and

---

WATER SHORTAGE

No matter how well behaved your dog is, bathing is always a project! Nothing can substitute for a good warm bath, but owners do have the option of giving their dogs "dry" baths. Pet shops sell excellent products, in both powder and spray forms, designed for spot-cleaning your dog. These dry shampoos are convenient for touch-up jobs when you don't have the time to bathe your dog in the traditional way.

Muddy feet, messy behinds and smelly coats can be spot-cleaned and deodorized with a "wet-nap"-style cleaner. On those days when your dog insists on rolling in fresh goose droppings and there's no time for a bath, a spot bath can save the day. These pre-moistened wipes are also handy for other grooming needs like wiping faces, ears and eyes and freshening tails and behinds.

blades on the top and bottom snip it off in one clip.

Start by grasping the pup's paw; a little pressure on the foot pad causes the nail to extend, making it easier to clip. Clip off a little at a time. If you can see the "quick," which is a blood vessel that runs through each nail, you will know how much to trim, as you do not want to cut into the quick. On that note, if you do cut the quick, which will cause bleeding, you can stem the flow of blood with a styptic pencil or other clotting agent. If you mistakenly nip the quick, do not panic or fuss, as this will cause the pup to be afraid. Simply reassure the pup, stop the bleeding and move on to the next nail. Don't be discouraged; you will become a professional canine pedicurist with practice.

You may or may not be able to see the quick, so it's best to just clip off a small bit at a time. If you see a dark dot in the center of the nail, this is the quick and your cue to stop clipping. Tell the puppy he's a "good boy" and offer a piece of treat with each nail. You can also use nail-clipping time to examine the footpads, making sure that they are not dry and cracked and that nothing has become embedded in them.

The nail grinder, the other choice, is many owners' first choice. Accustoming the puppy to the sound of the grinder and sensation of the buzz presents

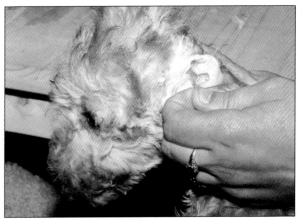

fewer challenges than the clipper, and there's no chance of cutting through the quick. Use the grinder on a low setting and always talk soothingly to your dog. He won't mind his salon visit, and he'll have nicely polished nails as well.

Part of keeping the ears clean is gently removing any excess hairs that grow inside the ears. The hairs can be plucked carefully, using your thumb and forefinger.

EAR CLEANING
While keeping your dog's ears clean unfortunately will not cause him to "hear" your commands any better, it will protect him from ear infection and ear-mite infestation. In addition, a dog's ears are vulnerable to waxy build-up and to collecting foreign matter from the outdoors. Look in your dog's ears regularly to ensure that they look pink, clean and otherwise healthy. Even if they look fine, an odor in the ears signals a problem and means it's time to call the vet.

A dog's ears should be cleaned regularly; once a week is suggested, and you can do this along with

for this purpose. Look at the dog's eyes to make sure no debris has entered; dogs with large eyes and those who spend time outdoors are especially prone to this.

The signs of an eye infection are obvious: mucus, redness, puffi-

If you will use clippers to trim your dog's nails, purchase ones made for dogs.

your regular brushing. Using a cotton ball or pad, and never probing into the ear canal, wipe the ear gently. You can use an ear-cleansing liquid or powder available from your vet or pet-supply store; alternatively, you might prefer to use homemade solutions with ingredients like one part white vinegar and one part hydrogen peroxide. Ask your vet about home remedies before you attempt to concoct something on your own!

Keep your dog's ears free of excess hair by plucking it as needed. If done gently, this will be painless for the dog. Look for wax, brown droppings (a sign of ear mites), redness or any other abnormalities. At the first sign of a problem, contact your vet so that he can prescribe an appropriate medication.

EYE CARE

During grooming sessions, pay extra attention to the condition of your dog's eyes. If the area around the eyes is soiled or if tear staining has occurred, there are various cleaning agents made especially

---

THE MONTHLY GRIND

If your dog doesn't like the feeling of nail clippers or if you're not comfortable using them, you may wish to try an electric nail grinder. This tool has a small sandpaper disc on the end that rotates to grind the nails down. Some feel that using a grinder reduces the risk of cutting into the quick; this can be true if the tool is used properly. Usually you will be able to tell where the quick is before you get to it. A benefit of the grinder is that it creates a smooth finish on the nails so that there are no ragged edges.

Because the tool makes noise, your dog should be introduced to it before the actual grinding takes place. Turn it on and let your dog hear the noise; turn it off and let him inspect it with you holding it. Use the grinder gently, holding it firmly and progressing a little at a time until you reach the proper length. Look at the nail as you grind so that you do not go too short. Stop at any indication that you are nearing the quick. It will take a few sessions for both you and the puppy to get used to the grinder. Make sure that you don't let his hair get tangled in the grinder!

ness, scabs or other signs of irritation. If your dog's eyes become infected, the vet will likely prescribe an antibiotic ointment for treatment. If you notice signs of more serious problems, such as opacities in the eye, which usually indicate cataracts, consult the vet at once. Taking time to pay attention to your dog's eyes will alert you in the early stages of any problem so that you can get your dog treatment as soon as possible. You could save your dog's sight!

IDENTIFICATION AND TRAVEL

ID FOR YOUR DOG

You love your Bedlington Terrier and want to keep him safe. Of course you take every precaution to prevent his escaping from the yard or becoming lost or stolen. You have a sturdy high fence and you always keep your dog on lead when out and about in public places. If your dog is not properly identified, however, you are overlooking a major aspect of his safety. We hope to never be in a situation where our dog is missing, but we should practice prevention in the unfortunate case that this happens; identification greatly increases the chances of your dog's being returned to you.

There are several ways to identify your dog. First, the traditional dog tag should be a staple in your dog's wardrobe, attached to his everyday collar. Tags can be made

PET OR STRAY?
Besides the obvious benefit of providing your contact information to whoever finds your lost dog, an ID tag makes your dog more approachable and more likely to be recovered. A strange dog wandering the neighborhood without a collar and tags will look like a stray, while the collar and tags indicate that the dog is someone's pet. Even if the ID tags become detached from the collar, the collar alone will make a person more likely to pick up the dog.

of sturdy plastic and various metals and should include your contact information so that a person who finds the dog can get in touch with you right away to arrange his return. Many people today enjoy the wide range of decorative tags available, so have fun and create a tag to match your dog's personality. Of course, it is important that the tag stays on the collar, so have a secure "O" ring attachment; you also can explore the type of tag that slides right onto the collar.

In addition to the ID tag, which every dog should wear even if identified by another method, two other forms of identification have become popular: microchipping and tattooing. In microchipping, a tiny scannable chip is painlessly inserted under the dog's skin. The number is registered to

You should research boarding kennels prior to your actually needing one. Meet the staff, see the facilities and discuss such things as costs, feeding, exercise, medical care, etc.

you so that, if your lost dog turns up at a clinic or shelter, the chip can be scanned to retrieve your contact information.

The advantage of the microchip is that it is a permanent form of ID, but there are some factors to consider. Several different companies make microchips, and not all are compatible with the others' scanning devices. It's best to find a company with a universal microchip that can be read by scanners made by other companies as well. It won't do any good to have the dog chipped if the information cannot be retrieved. Also, not every humane society, shelter and clinic is equipped with a scanner, although more and more facilities are equipping themselves. In fact, many shelters microchip dogs that they adopt out to new homes.

In the US, there are five or six major microchip manufacturers as well as a few databases. The American Kennel Club's Companion Animal Recovery unit

works in conjunction with HomeAgain™ Companion Animal Retrieval System (Schering-Plough). In the UK, The Kennel Club is affiliated with the National Pet Register, operated by Wood Green Animal Shelters.

Because the microchip is not visible to the eye, the dog must wear a tag that states that he is microchipped so that whoever picks him up will know to have him scanned. He of course also should have a tag with your contact information in case his chip cannot be read. Humane societies and veterinary clinics offer microchipping service, which is usually very affordable.

Though less popular than microchipping, tattooing is another permanent method of ID for dogs. Most vets perform this service, and there are also clinics that perform dog tattooing. This is also an affordable procedure and one that will not cause much discomfort for the dog. It is best to put the tattoo in a visible area, such as the ear, to deter theft. It is sad to say that there are cases of dogs' being stolen and sold to research laboratories, but such laboratories will not accept tattooed dogs.

To ensure that the tattoo is effective in aiding your dog's return to you, the tattoo number must be registered with a national organization. That way, when someone finds a tattooed dog, a phone call to the registry will quickly match the dog with his owner.

HIT THE ROAD

Car travel with your Bedlington Terrier may be limited to necessity only, such as trips to the vet, or you may bring your dog along almost everywhere you go. This will depend much on your individual dog and how he reacts to rides in the car. You can begin desensitizing your dog to car travel as a pup so that it's something that he's used to. Still, some dogs suffer from motion sickness. Your vet may prescribe a medication for this if trips in the car pose a problem for your dog. At the very least, you will need to get him to the vet, so he will need to tolerate these trips with the least amount of hassle possible.

Start taking your pup on short trips, maybe just around the block to start. If he is fine with short trips, lengthen your rides a little at a time. Start to take him on your errands or just for drives around town. By this time it will be easy to tell whether your dog is a born traveler or would prefer staying at home when you are on the road.

Of course, safety is a concern for dogs in the car. First, he must travel securely, not left loose to roam about the car where he could be injured or distract the driver. A young pup can be held by a passenger initially but should soon graduate to a travel crate, which

> **DOGGONE!**
> Wendy Ballard is the editor and publisher of the *DogGone*™ newsletter, which comes out bi-monthly and features fun articles by dog owners who love to travel with their dogs. The newsletter includes information about fun places to go with your dogs, including popular vacation spots, dog-friendly hotels, parks, campgrounds, resorts, etc., as well as interesting activities to do with your dog, such as flyball, agility and much more. You can subscribe to the publication by contacting the publisher at PO Box 651155, Vero Beach, FL 32965-1155.

can be the same crate he uses in the home. Other options include a car harness (like a seat belt for dogs) and partitioning the back of the car with a gate made for this purpose.

Bring along what you will need for the dog. He should wear his collar and ID tags, of course, and you should bring his leash, water (and food if a long trip) and clean-up materials for potty breaks and in case of motion sickness. Always keep your dog on his leash when you make stops, and never leave him alone in the car. Many a dog has died from the heat inside a closed car; this does not take much time at all. A dog left alone inside a car can also be a target for thieves.

TRAINING YOUR

BEDLINGTON TERRIER

BASIC TRAINING PRINCIPLES: PUPPY VS. ADULT

There's a big difference between training an adult dog and training a young puppy. With a young puppy, everything is new. At eight to ten weeks of age, he will be experiencing many things, and he has nothing with which to compare these experiences. Up to this point, he has been with his dam and littermates, not one-on-one with people except in his interactions with his breeder and visitors to the litter.

When you first bring the puppy home, he is eager to please you. This means that he accepts doing things your way. During the next couple of months, he will absorb the basis of everything he needs to know for the rest of his life. This early age is even referred to as the "sponge" stage. After that, for the next 18 months, it's up to you to reinforce good manners by building on the foundation that you've established. Once your puppy is reliable in basic commands and behavior and has reached the appropriate age, you may gradually introduce him to some of the interesting sports, games and activities available to pet owners and their dogs.

Raising your puppy is a family affair. Each member of the family must know what rules to set forth for the puppy and how to use the same one-word commands to mean exactly the same thing every time. Even if yours is a large family, one person will soon be considered by the pup to be the leader, the alpha person in his pack, the "boss" who must be obeyed. Often that highly regarded person turns out to be the one who feeds the puppy. Food ranks very high on the puppy's list of important things! That's why your puppy is rewarded with small treats along with verbal praise when he responds to you correctly. As the puppy learns to do what you want him to do, the food rewards are gradually eliminated and only the praise remains. If you were to keep up with the food treats, you could have two problems on your hands—an obese dog and a beggar.

An intelligent and quick breed, the Bedlington Terrier can be trained to respond to a multitude of commands and tricks—but it doesn't hurt to have a treat on hand!

Training begins the minute your Bedlington Terrier puppy steps through the doorway of your home, so don't make the mistake of putting the puppy on the floor and telling him by your actions to "Go for it! Run wild!" Even if this is your first puppy, you must act as if you know what you're doing: be the boss. An uncertain pup may be terrified to move, while a bold one will be ready to take you at your word and start plotting to destroy the house! Before you collected your puppy, you decided where his own special place would be, and that's where to put him when you first arrive home. Give him a house tour after he has investigated his area and

"SCHOOL" MODE

When is your puppy ready for a lesson? Maybe not always when you are. Attempting training with treats just before his mealtime is asking for disaster. Notice what times of day he performs best and make that Fido's school time.

had a nap and a bathroom "pit stop."

It's worth mentioning here that if you've adopted an adult dog that is completely trained to

OUR CANINE KIDS

"Everything I learned about parenting, I learned from my dog." How often adults recognize that their parenting skills are mere extensions of the education they acquired while caring for their dogs. Many owners refer to their dogs as their "kids" and treat their canine companions like real members of the family. Surveys indicate that a majority of dog owners talk to their dogs regularly, celebrate their dogs' birthdays and purchase Christmas gifts for their dogs. Another survey shows that dog owners take their dogs to the veterinarian more frequently than they visit their own physicians.

your liking, lucky you! You're off the hook! However, if that dog spent his life up to this point in a kennel, or even in a good home but without any real training, be prepared to tackle the job ahead. A dog three years of age or older with no previous training cannot be blamed for not knowing what he was never taught. While the dog is trying to understand and learn your rules, at the same time he has to unlearn many of his previously self-taught habits and general view of the world.

Working with a professional trainer will speed up your progress with an adopted adult dog. You'll need patience, too. Some new rules may be close to impossible for the dog to accept. After all, he's been successful so far by doing everything his way! (Patience again.) He may agree with your instruction for a few days and then slip back into his old ways, so you must be just as consistent and understanding in your teaching as you would be with a puppy. (More patience needed yet again!) Your dog has to learn to pay attention to your voice, your family, the daily routine, new smells, new sounds and, in some cases, even a new climate.

One of the most important things to find out about a newly adopted adult dog is his reaction to children (yours and others), strangers and your friends, and

CANINE DEVELOPMENT SCHEDULE

It is important to understand how and at what age a puppy develops into adulthood. If you are a puppy owner, consult this Canine Development Schedule to determine the stage of development your puppy is currently experiencing. This knowledge will help you as you work with the puppy in the weeks and months ahead.

PERIOD	AGE	CHARACTERISTICS
FIRST TO THIRD	BIRTH TO SEVEN WEEKS	Puppy needs food, sleep and warmth and responds to simple and gentle touching. Needs mother for security and disciplining. Needs littermates for learning and interacting with other dogs. Pup learns to function within a pack and learns pack order of dominance. Begin socializing pup with adults and children for short periods. Pup begins to become aware of his environment.
FOURTH	EIGHT TO TWELVE WEEKS	Brain is fully developed. Pup needs socializing with outside world. Remove from mother and littermates. Needs to change from canine pack to human pack. Human dominance necessary. Fear period occurs between 8 and 12 weeks. Avoid fright and pain.
FIFTH	THIRTEEN TO SIXTEEN WEEKS	Training and formal obedience should begin. Less association with other dogs, more with people, places, situations. Period will pass easily if you remember this is pup's change-to-adolescence time. Be firm and fair. Flight instinct prominent. Permissiveness and over-disciplining can do permanent damage. Praise for good behavior.
JUVENILE	FOUR TO EIGHT MONTHS	Another fear period about seven to eight months of age. It passes quickly, but be cautious of fright and pain. Sexual maturity reached. Dominant traits established. Dog should understand sit, down, come and stay by now.

NOTE: THESE ARE APPROXIMATE TIME FRAMES. ALLOW FOR INDIVIDUAL DIFFERENCES IN PUPPIES.

how he acts upon meeting other dogs. If he was not socialized with dogs as a puppy, this could be a major problem. This does not mean that he's a "bad" dog, a vicious dog or an aggressive dog; rather, it means that he has no idea how to read another dog's body language. There's no way for him to tell whether the other dog is a friend or foe. Survival instinct takes over, telling him to attack first and ask questions later. This definitely calls for professional help and, even then, may not be a behavior that can be corrected 100% reliably (or even at all). If you have a puppy, this is why it is so very important to introduce your young puppy properly to other puppies and "dog-friendly" adult dogs.

A properly trained and socialized Bedlington should have no problem sharing a meal with a friend. Any aggressive behavior toward other dogs should be cause for concern.

SMILE WHEN YOU ORDER ME AROUND!

While trainers recommend practicing with your dog every day, it's perfectly acceptable to take a "mental health day" off. It's better not to train the dog on days when you're in a sour mood. Your bad attitude or lack of interest will be sensed by your dog, and he will respond accordingly. Studies show that dogs are well tuned in to their humans' emotions. Be conscious of how you use your voice when talking to your dog. Raising your voice or shouting will only erode your dog's trust in you as his trainer and master.

HOUSE-TRAINING YOUR BEDLINGTON TERRIER

Dogs are tactility-oriented when it comes to house-training. In other words, they respond to the surface on which they are given approval to eliminate. The choice is yours (the dog's version is in parentheses): The lawn (including the neighbors' lawns)? A bare patch of earth under a tree (where people like to sit and relax in the summertime)? Concrete steps or patio (all sidewalks, garages and basement floors)? The curbside (watch out for cars)? A small area of crushed stone in a corner of the yard (mine!)? The latter is the best choice if you can manage it, because it will remain strictly for the dog's use and is easy to keep clean.

You can start out with paper-training indoors and switch over to an outdoor surface as the puppy matures and gains control over his need to eliminate. For the nay-sayers, don't worry—this won't mean that the dog will soil on every piece of newspaper lying around the house. You are training him to go outside, remember? Starting out by paper-training often is the only choice for a city dog.

WHEN YOUR PUPPY'S "GOT TO GO"
Your puppy's need to relieve himself is seemingly non-stop, but signs of improvement will be seen each week. From 8 to 10 weeks old, the puppy will have to be taken outside every time he wakes

EXTRA! EXTRA!
The headlines read: "Puppy Piddles Here!" Breeders commonly use newspapers to line their whelping pens, so puppies learn to associate newspapers with relieving themselves. Do not use newspapers to line your pup's crate, as this will signal to your puppy that it is OK to urinate in his crate. If you choose to paper-train your puppy, you will layer newspapers on a section of the floor near the door he uses to go outside. You should encourage the puppy to use the papers to relieve himself, and bring him there whenever you see him getting ready to go. Little by little, you will reduce the size of the newspaper-covered area so that the puppy will learn to relieve himself "on the other side of the door."

Crates made of wire are popular for use in the home. With a Bedlington, who loves to be part of the action, the wire crate allows him to see all that's going on around him.

up, about 10 to 15 minutes after every meal and after every period of play—all day long, from first thing in the morning until his bedtime! That's a total of ten or more trips per day to teach the puppy where it's okay to relieve himself. With that schedule in mind, you can see that house-training a young puppy is not a part-time job. It requires someone to be home all day.

If that seems overwhelming or impossible, do a little planning. For example, plan to pick up your puppy at the start of a vacation period. If you can't get home in the middle of the day, plan to hire a dog-sitter or ask a neighbor to come over to take the pup outside, feed him his lunch and then take him out again about ten or so minutes after he's eaten. Also make arrangements with that or

This puppy made it to the door, but the owner didn't get there in time. Your puppy will tell you through his behavior when it's time to go out—do not ignore the signs!

> ### SHOULD WE ENROLL?
> If you have the means and the time, you should definitely take your dog to obedience classes. Begin with puppy kindergarten classes in which puppies of all sizes learn basic lessons while getting the opportunity to meet and greet each other; it's as much about socialization as it is about good manners. What you learn in class you can practice at home. And if you goof up in practice, you'll get help in the next session.

another person to be your "emergency" contact if you have to stay late on the job. Remind yourself—repeatedly—that this hectic schedule improves as the puppy gets older.

HOME WITHIN A HOME
Your Bedlington Terrier puppy needs to be confined to one secure, puppy-proof area when no one is able to watch his every move. Generally the kitchen is the place of choice because the floor is washable. Likewise, it's a busy family area that will accustom the pup to a variety of noises, everything from pots and pans to the telephone, blender and dishwasher. He will also be enchanted by the smell of your cooking (and will never be critical when you burn something). An exercise pen (also called an "expen") within the room of choice

can be helpful in confining a young pup as long as he can't climb out! He can see out and has a certain amount of space in which to run about, but he is safe from dangerous things like electrical cords, heating units, trash baskets or open kitchen-supply cabinets. Place the pen where the puppy will not get a blast of heat or air conditioning.

In the pen, you can put a few toys, his bed (which can be his crate if the dimensions of pen and crate are compatible) and a few layers of newspaper in one small corner, just in case. A water bowl can be hung at a convenient height on the side of the ex-pen so it won't become a splashing pool for an innovative puppy. His food dish can go on the floor, near but not directly under the water bowl.

Crates are something that pet owners are at last getting used to for their dogs. Wild or domestic canines have always preferred to sleep in den-like safe spots, and that is exactly what the crate provides. How often have you seen adult dogs that choose to sleep under a table or chair even though they have full run of the house? It's the den connection.

In your "happy" voice, use the word "Crate" every time you put the pup into his den. If he's new to a crate, toss in a small biscuit for him to chase the first few times. At night, after he's been outside, he should sleep in his

TIDY BOY
Clean by nature, dogs do not like to soil their dens, which in effect are their crates or sleeping quarters. Unless not feeling well, dogs will not defecate or urinate in their crates. Crate training capitalizes on the dog's natural desire to keep his den clean. Be conscientious about giving the puppy as many opportunities to relieve himself outdoors as possible. Reward the puppy for correct behavior. Praise him and pat him whenever he "goes" in the correct location. Even the tidiest of puppies can have potty accidents, so be patient and dedicate more energy to helping your puppy achieve a clean lifestyle.

crate. The crate may be kept in his designated area at night or, if you want to be sure to hear those wake-up yips in the morning, put the crate in a corner of your bedroom. However, don't make any response whatsoever to

DAILY SCHEDULE

How many relief trips does your puppy need per day? A puppy up to the age of 14 weeks will need to go outside about 8 to 12 times per day! You will have to take the pup out any time he starts sniffing around the floor or turning in small circles, as well as after naps, meals, games and lessons or whenever he's released from his crate. Once the puppy is 14 to 22 weeks of age, he will require only 6 to 8 relief trips. At the ages of 22 to 32 weeks, the puppy will require about 5 to 7 trips. Adult dogs typically require 4 relief trips per day, in the morning, afternoon, evening and late at night.

whining or crying. If he's completely ignored, he'll settle down and get to sleep.

Good bedding for a young puppy is an old folded bath towel or an old blanket, something that is easily washable and disposable

if necessary ("accidents" will happen!). Never put newspaper in the puppy's crate. Also, those old ideas about adding a clock to replace his mother's heartbeat, or a hot-water bottle to replace her warmth, are just that—old ideas. The clock could drive the puppy nuts, and the hot-water bottle could end up as a very soggy waterbed! An extremely good breeder would have introduced your puppy to the crate by letting two pups sleep together for a couple of nights, followed by several nights alone. How thankful you will be if you found that breeder!

Safe toys in the pup's crate or area will keep him occupied, but monitor their condition closely. Discard any toys that show signs of being chewed to bits. Squeaky parts, bits of stuffing or plastic or any other small pieces can cause intestinal blockage or possibly choking if swallowed.

PROGRESSING WITH POTTY-TRAINING
After you've taken your puppy out and he has relieved himself in the area you've selected, he can have some free time with the family as long as there is someone responsible for watching him. That doesn't mean just someone in the same room who is watching TV or busy on the computer, but one person who is doing nothing other than keeping an eye on the pup, playing with him on the

floor and helping him understand his position in the pack.

This first taste of freedom will let you begin to set the house rules. If you don't want the dog on the furniture, now is the time to prevent his first attempts to jump up onto the couch. The word to use in this case is "Off," not "Down." "Down" is the word you will use to teach the down position, which is something entirely different.

Most corrections at this stage come in the form of simply distracting the puppy. Instead of

THE SUCCESS METHOD

Success that comes by luck is usually short-lived. Success that comes by well-thought-out proven methods is often more easily achieved and permanent. This is the Success Method. It is designed to give you, the puppy owner, a simple yet proven way to help your puppy develop clean living habits and a feeling of security in his new environment.

6 STEPS TO SUCCESSFUL CRATE TRAINING

1 Tell the puppy "Crate time!" and place him into the crate with a small treat (a piece of cheese or half of a biscuit). Let him stay in the crate for five minutes while you are in the same room. Then release him and praise. Never release him when he is fussing. Wait until he is quiet before you let him out.

2 Repeat Step 1 several times a day.

3 The next day, place the puppy into the crate as before. Let him stay there for ten minutes. Do this several times.

4 Continue building time in five-minute increments until the puppy stays in his crate for 30 minutes with you in the room. Always take him to his relief area after prolonged periods in his crate.

5 Now go back to Step 1 and let the puppy stay in his crate for five minutes, this time while you are out of the room.

6 Once again, build crate time in five-minute increments with you out of the room. When the puppy will stay willingly in his crate (he may even fall asleep!) for 30 minutes with you out of the room, he will be ready to stay in it for several hours at a time.

It won't take long for your pup to recognize his chosen relief spot. His nose will reliably lead him there time after time.

to take a small piece of soiled paper and place it in the middle of the new clean papers, as the scent will attract him to that spot when it's time to go again. That scent attraction is why it's so important to clean up any messes made in the house by using a product specially made to eliminate the odor of dog urine and droppings. Regular household cleansers won't do the trick. Pet shops sell the best pet deodorizers. Invest in the largest container you can find.

Scent attraction eventually will lead your pup to his chosen spot outdoors; this is the basis of outdoor training. When you take your puppy outside to relieve himself, use a one-word command such as "Outside" or "Go-potty" (that's one word to the puppy!) as you attach his leash. Then lead him to his spot. Now comes the hard part—hard

telling him "No" for "Don't chew the carpet," distract the chomping puppy with a toy and he'll forget about the carpet.

As you are playing with the pup, do not forget to watch him closely and pay attention to his body language. Whenever you see him begin to circle or sniff, take the puppy outside to relieve himself. If you are paper-training, put him back into his confined area on the newspapers. In either case, praise him as he eliminates while he actually is *in the act* of relieving himself. Three seconds after he has finished is too late! You'll be praising him for running toward you, picking up a toy or whatever he may be doing at that moment, and that's not what you want to be praising him for. Timing is a vital tool in all dog training. Use it.

Remove soiled newspapers immediately and replace them with clean ones. You may want

KEEP IT SIMPLE—AND FUN

Keep your lessons simple, interesting and user-friendly. Fun breaks help you both. Spend two minutes or ten teaching your puppy, but practice only as long as your dog enjoys what he's doing and is focused on pleasing you. If he's bored or distracted, stop the training session after any correct response (always end on a high note!). After a few minutes of playtime, you can go back to "hitting the books."

> **BE UPSTANDING!**
> You are the dog's leader. During training, stand up straight so your dog looks up at you, and therefore up *to* you. Say the command words distinctly, in a clear, declarative tone of voice. (No barking!) Give rewards only as the correct response takes place (remember your timing!). Praise, smiles and treats are "rewards" used to positively reinforce correct responses. Don't repeat a mistake. Just change to another exercise—you will soon find success!

for you, that is. Just stand there until he urinates and defecates. Move him a few feet in one direction or another if he's just sitting there looking at you, but remember that this is neither playtime nor time for a walk. This is strictly a business trip! Then, as he circles and squats (remember your timing!), give him a quiet "Good dog" as praise. If you start to jump for joy, ecstatic over his performance, he'll do one of two things: either he will stop midstream, as it were, or he'll do it again for you—in the house—and expect you to be just as delighted!

Give him five minutes or so and, if he doesn't go in that time, take him back indoors to his confined area and try again in another ten minutes, or immediately if you see him sniffing and

circling. By careful observation, you'll soon work out a successful schedule.

Accidents, by the way, are just that—accidents. Clean them up quickly and thoroughly, without comment, after the puppy has been taken outside to finish his business and then put back into his area or crate. If you witness an accident in progress, say "No!" in a stern voice and get the pup outdoors immediately. No punishment is needed. You and your puppy are just learning each other's language, and sometimes it's easy to miss a puppy's message. Chalk it up to experience and watch more closely from now on.

KEEPING THE PACK ORDERLY
Discipline is a form of training that brings order to life. For example, military discipline is what allows the soldiers in an army to work as one. Discipline is a form of teaching and, in dogs, is the basis of how the successful pack operates. Each member knows his place in the pack and all respect the leader, or alpha dog. It is essential for your puppy that you establish this type of relationship, with you as the alpha, or leader. It is a form of social coexistence that all canines recognize and accept. Discipline, therefore, is never to be confused with punishment. When you teach your puppy how you want

WHO'S TRAINING WHOM?

Dog training is a black-and-white exercise. The correct response to a command must be absolute, and the trainer must insist on completely accurate responses from the dog. A trainer cannot command his dog to sit and then settle for the dog's melting into the down position. Often owners are so pleased that their dogs "did something" in response to a command that they just shrug and say, "OK, down" even though they wanted the dog to sit. You want your dog to respond to the command without hesitation: he must respond at that moment and correctly every time.

him to behave, and he behaves properly and you praise him for it, you are disciplining him with a form of positive reinforcement.

For a dog, rewards come in the form of praise, a smile, a cheerful tone of voice, a few friendly pats or a rub of the ears. Rewards are also small food treats. Obviously, that does not mean bits of regular dog food. Instead, treats are very small bits of special things like cheese or pieces of soft dog treats. The idea is to reward the dog with something very small that he can taste and swallow, providing instant positive reinforcement. If he has to take time to chew the treat, he will have forgotten what he did to earn it by the time he is finished!

Your puppy should never be physically punished. The displeasure shown on your face and in your voice is sufficient to signal to the pup that he has done something wrong. He wants to please everyone higher up on the social ladder, especially his leader, so a scowl and harsh voice will take care of the error. Growling out the word "Shame!" when the pup is caught in the act of doing something wrong is better than the repetitive "No." Some dogs hear "No" so often that they begin to think it's their name! By the way, do not use the dog's name when you're correcting him. His name is reserved to get his attention for something pleasant about to take place.

There are punishments that have nothing to do with you. For example, your dog may think that chasing cats is one reason for his existence. You can try to stop it as much as you like but without success, because it's such fun for the dog. But one good hissing, spitting swipe of a cat's claws across the dog's nose will put an end to the game forever. Intervene only when your dog's eyeball is seriously at risk. Cat scratches can cause permanent damage to an innocent but annoying puppy.

PUPPY KINDERGARTEN

COLLAR AND LEASH

Before you begin your Bedlington Terrier puppy's education, he must be used to his collar and leash. Choose a collar for your puppy that is secure, but not heavy or bulky. He won't enjoy training if he's uncomfortable. A flat buckle collar is fine for everyday wear and for initial puppy training. For older dogs, there are several types of training collars such as the martingale, which is a double loop that tightens slightly around the neck, or the head collar, which is similar to a horse's halter. Ask your breeder or a trainer if he recommends a training collar and, if so, what type. With any type of training collar, you must know

how to put it on your dog and use it properly.

A lightweight 6-foot woven cotton or nylon training leash is preferred by most trainers because it is easy to fold up in your hand and comfortable to hold because there is a certain amount of give to it. There are lessons where the dog will start off 6 feet away from you at the end of the leash. The leash used to take the puppy outside to relieve himself is shorter because you don't want him to roam away from his area. The shorter leash will also be the one to use when you walk the puppy.

If you've been wise enough to enroll in a puppy kindergarten training class, suggestions will be made as to the best collar and leash for your young puppy. I say

BASIC PRINCIPLES OF DOG TRAINING

1. Start training early. A young puppy is ready, willing and able.
2. Timing is your all-important tool. Praise at the exact time that the dog responds correctly. Pay close attention.
3. Patience is almost as important as timing!
4. Repeat! The same word has to mean the same thing every time.
5. In the beginning, praise all correct behavior verbally, along with treats and petting.

"wise" because your puppy will be in a class with puppies in his age range (up to five months old) of all breeds and sizes. It's the perfect

LEADER OF THE PACK

Canines are pack animals. They live according to pack rules, and every pack has only one leader. Guess what? That's you! To establish your position of authority, lay down the rules and be fair and good-natured in all your dealings with your dog. He will consider young children as his littermates, but the one who trains him, who feeds him, who grooms him, who expects him to come into line, that's his leader. And he who leads must be obeyed.

way for him to learn the right way (and the wrong way) to interact with other dogs as well as their people. You cannot teach your puppy how to interpret another dog's sign language. For a first-time puppy owner, these socialization classes are invaluable. For experienced dog owners, they are a real boon to further training.

ATTENTION

You've been using the dog's name since the minute you collected him from the breeder, so you should be able to get his attention by saying his name—with a big smile and in an excited tone of voice. His response will be the puppy equivalent of "Here I am! What are we going to do?" Your immediate response (if you haven't guessed by now) is "Good dog." Rewarding him at the moment he pays attention to you teaches him the proper way to respond when he hears his name.

EXERCISES FOR A BASIC CANINE EDUCATION

THE SIT EXERCISE

There are several ways to teach the puppy to sit. The first one is to catch him whenever he is about to sit and, as his backside nears the floor, say "Sit, good dog!" That's positive reinforcement and, if your timing is sharp, he will learn that what he's doing at that second is connected to your saying "Sit" and that you think he's clever for doing it!

Another method is to start with the puppy on his leash in front of you. Show him a treat in the palm of your right hand. Bring your hand up under his nose and, almost in slow motion, move your hand up and back so his nose goes up in the air and his head tilts back as he follows the treat in your hand. At that point, he will have to either sit or fall over, so as his back legs buckle under, say "Sit, good dog," and then give him the treat and lots of praise. You may have to begin with your hand lightly running up his chest, actually lifting his chin up until he sits. Some (usually older) dogs require gentle pressure on their hindquarters with the left hand, in which case the dog should be on your left side. Puppies gener-

CREATURES OF HABIT

Canine behaviorists and trainers aptly describe dogs as "creatures of habit," meaning that dogs respond to structure in their daily lives and welcome a routine. Do not interpret this to mean that dogs enjoy endless repetition in their training sessions. Dogs get bored just as humans do. Keep training sessions interesting and exciting. Vary the commands and the locations in which you practice. Give short breaks for play in between lessons. A bored student will never be the best performer in the class.

ally do not appreciate this physical dominance.

After a few times, you should be able to show the dog a treat in the open palm of your hand, raise your hand waist-high as you say "Sit" and have him sit. You thereby will have taught him two things at the same time. Both the verbal command and the motion of the hand are signals for the sit. Your puppy is watching you almost more than he is listening

You should have no problem teaching your Bedlington to sit. This basic command is one of the first that every dog learns.

DOWN

"Down" is a harsh-sounding word and a submissive posture in dog body language, thus presenting two obstacles in teaching the down command. When the dog is about to flop down on his own, tell him "Good down." Pups that are not good about being handled learn better by having food lowered in front of them. A dog that trusts you can be gently guided into position. When you give the command "Down," be sure to say it sweetly!

to you, so what you do is just as important as what you say.

Don't save any of these drills only for training sessions. Use them as much as possible at odd times during a normal day. The dog should always sit before being given his food dish. He should sit to let you go through a doorway first, when the doorbell rings or when you stop to speak to someone on the street.

THE DOWN EXERCISE

Before beginning to teach the down command, you must consider how the dog feels about this exercise. To him, "down" is a submissive position. Being flat on the floor with you standing over him is not his idea of fun. It's up to you to let him know that, while it may not be fun, the reward of your approval is worth his effort.

Start with the puppy on your left side in a sit position. Hold the leash right above his collar in your left hand. Have an extra-special treat, such as a small piece of cooked chicken or hot dog, in your right hand. Place it at the end of the pup's nose and steadily move your hand down and forward along the ground. Hold the leash to prevent a sudden lunge for the food. As the puppy goes into the down position, say "Down" very gently.

The difficulty with this exercise is twofold: it's both the submissive aspect and the fact that most people say the word "Down" as if they were drill sergeants in charge of recruits! So issue the command sweetly, give him the treat and have the pup maintain the down position for several seconds. If he tries to get up immediately, place your hands on his shoulders and press down gently, giving him a very quiet "Good dog." As you progress with this lesson, increase the "down time" until he will hold it until

level in your left hand and let the dog know that you have a treat in your closed right hand. Step forward on your right foot as you say "Stay." Immediately turn and stand directly in front of the dog, keeping your right hand up high so he'll keep his eye on the treat hand and maintain the sit position for a count of five. Return to your original position and offer the reward.

Increase the length of the sit/stay each time until the dog can hold it for at least 30 seconds

You can use hand signals along with your verbal commands when teaching your Bedlington.

you say "Okay" (his cue for release). Practice this one in the house at various times throughout the day.

By increasing the length of time during which the dog must maintain the down position, you'll find many uses for it. For example, he can lie at your feet in the vet's office or anywhere that both of you have to wait, when you are on the phone, while the family is eating and so forth. If you progress to training for competitive obedience, he'll already be all set for the exercise called the "long down."

THE STAY EXERCISE

You can teach your Bedlington Terrier to stay in the sit, down and stand positions. To teach the sit/stay, have the dog sit on your left side. Hold the leash at waist

SAY IT SIMPLY

When you command your dog to sit, use the word "Sit." Do not say "Sit down," as your dog will not know whether you mean "Sit" or "Down," or maybe you mean both. Be clear in your instructions to your dog; use one-word commands and always be consistent.

TIPS FOR TRAINING AND SAFETY

1. Whether on- or off-leash, practice only in a fenced area.
2. Remove the training collar when the training session is over.
3. Don't try to break up a dogfight.
4. "Come," "Leave it" and "Wait" are safety commands.
5. The dog belongs in a crate or behind a barrier when riding in the car.
6. Don't ignore the dog's first sign of aggression. Aggression only gets worse, so take it seriously.
7. Keep the faces of children and dogs separated.
8. Pay attention to what the dog is chewing.
9. Keep the vet's number near your phone.
10. "Okay" is a useful release command.

upset by having to back up for a few days. The repetition and practice are what will make your dog reliable in these commands. It won't do any good to move on to something more difficult if the command is not mastered at the easier levels. Above all, even if you do get frustrated, never let your puppy know! Always keep a positive, upbeat attitude during training, which will transmit to your dog for positive results.

The down/stay is taught in the same way once the dog is completely reliable and steady with the down command. Again, don't rush it. With the dog in the down position on your left side, step out on your right foot as you say "Stay." Return by walking around in back of the dog and into your original position. While you are training, it's okay to murmur something like "Hold on" to encourage him to stay put. When the dog will stay without moving when you are at a distance of 3 or 4 feet, begin to increase the length of time before you return. Be sure he holds the down on your return until you say "Okay." At that point, he gets his treat—just so he'll remember for next time that it's not over until it's over.

THE COME EXERCISE

No command is more important to the safety of your Bedlington Terrier than "Come." It is what you

without moving. After about a week of success, move out on your right foot and take two steps before turning to face the dog. Give the "Stay" hand signal (left palm back toward the dog's head) as you leave. He gets the treat when you return and he holds the sit/stay. Increase the distance that you walk away from him before turning until you reach the length of your training leash. But don't rush it! Go back to the beginning if he moves before he should. No matter what the lesson, never be should say every single time you see the puppy running toward you: "Stuart, come! Good dog." During playtime, run a few feet away from the puppy and turn and tell him to "Come" as he is already running to you. You can go so far as to teach your puppy two things at once if you squat down and hold out your arms. As the pup gets close to you and you're saying "Good dog," bring your right arm in about waist high. Now he's also learning the hand signal, an excellent device should you be on the phone when you need to get him to come to you! You'll also both be one step ahead when you enter obedience classes.

When the puppy responds to your well-timed "Come," try it with the puppy on the training leash. This time, catch him off guard, while he's sniffing a leaf or watching a bird: "Stuart, come!" You may have to pause for a split second after his name to be sure you have his attention. If the puppy shows any sign of confusion, give the leash a mild jerk and take a couple of steps backward. Do not repeat the command. In this case, you should say "Good come" as he reaches you.

That's the number-one rule of training. Each command word is given just once. Anything more is nagging. You'll also notice that all commands are one word only. Even when they are actually two words, you say them as one.

Never call the dog to come to you—with or without his name—if you are angry or intend to correct him for some misbehavior. When correcting the pup, you go to him. Your dog must always connect "Come" with something pleasant and with your approval; then you can rely on his response.

Puppies, like children, have notoriously short attention spans, so don't overdo it with any of the training. Keep each lesson short. Break it up with a quick run around the yard or a ball toss, repeat the lesson and quit as soon as the pup gets it right. That way, you will always end with a "Good dog."

Life isn't perfect and neither are puppies. A time will come, often around ten months of age, when he'll become "selectively deaf" or choose to "forget" his

READY, SIT, GO!
On your marks, get set: train! Most professional trainers agree that the sit command is the place to start your dog's formal education. Sitting is a natural posture for most dogs, and they respond to the sit exercise willingly and readily. For every lesson, begin with the sit command so that you start out with a successful exercise; likewise, you should practice the sit command at the end of every lesson as well because you always want to end on a high note.

throw his favorite toy and skip the lesson you had planned. Pups will be pups!

THE HEEL EXERCISE

The second most important command to teach, after the come, is the heel. When you are walking your growing puppy, you need to be in control. Besides, it looks terrible to be pulled and yanked down the street, and it's not much fun either. Your eight- to ten-week-old puppy will probably follow you everywhere, but that's his natural instinct, not your control over the situation. However, any time he does follow you, you can say "Heel" and be ahead of the game, as he will learn to associate this command with the action of following you before you even begin teaching him to heel.

There is a very precise, almost military, procedure for teaching your dog to heel. As with all other obedience training, begin with the dog on your left side. He will be in a very nice sit and you will have the training leash across your chest. Hold the loop and folded leash in your right hand. Pick up the slack leash above the dog in your left hand and hold it loosely at your side. Step out on your left foot as you say "Heel." If the puppy does not move, give a gentle tug or pat your left leg to get him started. If he surges ahead of you, stop and pull him back gently until he is at your side. Tell

LET'S GO!

Many people use "Let's go" instead of "Heel" when teaching their dogs to behave on lead. It sounds more like fun! When beginning to teach the heel, whatever command you use, always step off on your left foot. That's the one next to the dog, who is on your left side, in case you've forgotten. Keep a loose leash. When the dog pulls ahead, stop, bring him back and begin again. Use treats to guide him around turns.

name. He may respond by wagging his tail (and even seeming to smile at you) with a look that says "Make me!" Laugh,

COME AND GET IT!

The come command is your dog's safety signal. Until he is 99% perfect in responding, don't use the come command if you cannot enforce it. Practice on leash with treats or squeakers, or whenever the dog is running to you. Never call him to come to you if he is to be corrected for a misdemeanor. Reward the dog with a treat and happy praise whenever he comes to you.

him to sit and begin again.

Walk a few steps and stop while the puppy is correctly beside you. Tell him to sit and give mild verbal praise. (More enthusiastic praise will encourage him to think the lesson is over.) Repeat the lesson, increasing the number of steps you take only as long as the dog is heeling nicely beside you. When you end the lesson, have him hold the sit, then give him the "Okay" to let him know that this is the end of the lesson. Praise him so that he knows he did a good job.

The cure for excessive pulling (a common problem) is to stop when the dog is no more than 2 or 3 feet ahead of you. Guide him back into position and begin again. With a really determined puller, try switching to a head collar. When used correctly, this will automatically turn the pup's head toward you so you can bring him

back easily to the heel position. Give quiet, reassuring praise every time the leash goes slack and he's staying with you.

Staying and heeling can take a lot out of a dog, so provide playtime and free-running exercise to shake off the stress when the lessons are over. You don't want him to associate training with all work and no fun.

TAPERING OFF TIDBITS

Your dog has been watching you—and the hand that treats—throughout all of his lessons, and now it's time to break the treat habit. Begin by giving him treats at the end of each lesson only. Then start to give a treat after the end of only some of the lessons. At the end of every lesson, as well as during the lessons, be consistent with the praise. Your pup now doesn't

Heeling is basic "good manners" for all dogs, pet or show. This show dog must heel next to his handler as the judge evaluates his gait.

The compact size and friendly disposition of the Bedlington Terrier make him an ideal candidate for therapy work. This lovely lady is enjoying her canine visit.

know whether he'll get a treat or not, but he should keep performing well just in case! Finally, you will stop giving treat rewards entirely. Save them for something brand-new that you want to teach him. Keep up the praise and you'll always have a "good dog."

OBEDIENCE CLASSES

The advantages of an obedience class are that your dog will have to learn amid the distractions of other people and dogs and that your mistakes will be quickly corrected by the trainer. Teaching your dog along with a qualified instructor and other handlers who may have more dog experience than you is another plus of the class environment. The instructor and other handlers can help you to find the most efficient way of teaching your dog a command or exercise. It's often easier to learn

by other people's mistakes than your own. You will also learn all of the requirements for competitive obedience trials, in which you can earn titles and go on to advanced jumping and retrieving exercises, which are fun for many dogs. Obedience classes build the foundation needed for many other canine activities (in which we humans are allowed to participate, too!).

TRAINING FOR OTHER ACTIVITIES

Once your dog has basic obedience under his collar and is 12 months of age, you can enter the world of agility training. Dogs think agility is pure fun, like being turned loose in an amusement park full of obstacles! In addition to agility, there are hunting activities for sporting dogs, lure-coursing events for sighthounds, go-to-ground events for terriers, racing for the Nordic sled dogs, herding trials for the shepherd breeds and tracking, which is open to all "nosey" dogs (which would include all dogs!). For those who like to volunteer, there is the wonderful feeling of owning a therapy dog and visiting hospices, nursing homes and veterans' homes to bring smiles, comfort and companionship to those who live there.

Around the house, your Bedlington Terrier can be taught to do some simple chores. You might teach him to carry small household items or fetch the morning newspaper. The kids can teach the dog all kinds of tricks, from playing hide-and-seek to balancing a biscuit on his nose. A family dog is what rounds out the family. Everything he does, including sitting in your lap and gazing lovingly at you, represents the bonus of owning a dog.

If you are interested in participating in organized competition with your Bedlington Terrier, there are activities other than obedience in which you and your dog can become involved. Going-to-ground activities are every Bedlington's favorite outing, and owners should investigate earthdog trials sponsored by local terrier clubs. The American Working Terrier Association was founded in 1971 to encourage and preserve the natural instinct of earth terriers. The dogs are to enter an underground tunnel and to react in a positive manner when facing the quarry. A Working Certificate is issued to dogs who qualify for working in a natural den. The AWTA issues Working, Hunting and Gameness Certificates. The AKC also sponsors earthdog events and awards titles.

Agility is a popular sport in which dogs run through an obstacle course that includes various jumps, tunnels and other exercises to test the dog's speed and coordination. Dogs of all sizes can compete, as obstacles are adjusted to different height classes. The owners run beside their dogs to give commands and to guide them through the course. Although competitive, the focus is on fun—it's fun to do, fun to watch and great exercise.

Flyball, which began as an American sport in California in the 1970s, has become popular in some canine circles, and some Bedlingtons have applied their lithe bodies to the sport and won titles. In effect, flyball is a relay race where four dogs jump over hurdles and then trigger a ball from a box, catch the ball and then "fly" back over the hurdles. It is entertaining for dogs, owners and spectators and is growing in popularity every year.

Bedlingtons are agile, active, intelligent and ready to participate in most anything—a winning combination that makes him well suited to agility training.

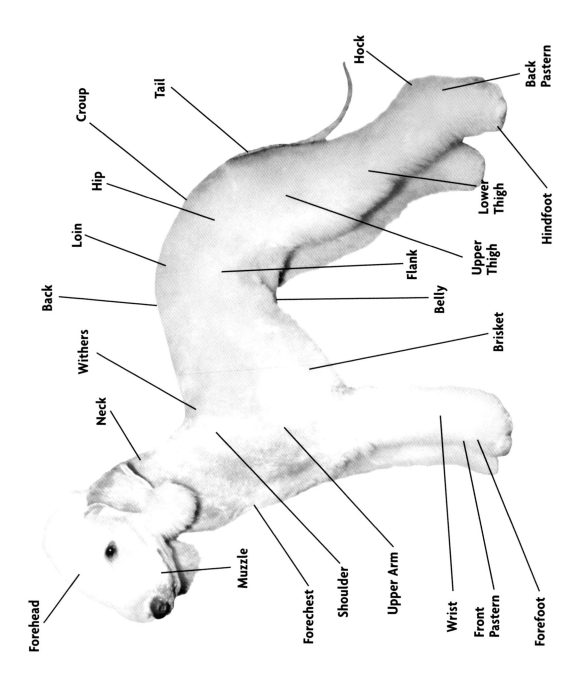

Forehead

Neck

Withers

Back

Loin

Hip

Croup

Tail

Hock

Back
Pastern

Hindfoot

Lower
Thigh

Upper
Thigh

Flank

Belly

Brisket

Muzzle

Forechest

Shoulder

Upper Arm

Wrist

Front
Pastern

Forefoot

PHYSICAL STRUCTURE OF THE BEDLINGTON TERRIER

HEALTHCARE OF YOUR
BEDLINGTON TERRIER

BY LOWELL ACKERMAN DVM, DACVD

HEALTHCARE FOR A LIFETIME

When you own a dog, you become his healthcare advocate over his entire lifespan, as well as being the one to shoulder the financial burden of such care. Accordingly, it is worthwhile to focus on prevention rather than treatment, as you and your pet will both be happier.

Of course, the best place to have begun your program of preventive healthcare is with the initial purchase or adoption of your dog. There is no way of guaranteeing that your new furry friend is free of medical problems, but there are some things you can do to improve your odds. You certainly should have done adequate research into the Bedlington Terrier and have selected your puppy carefully rather than buying on impulse. Health issues aside, a large number of pet abandonment and relinquishment cases arise from a mismatch between pet needs and owner expectations. This is entirely preventable with appropriate planning and finding a good breeder.

Regarding healthcare issues specifically, it is very difficult to make blanket statements about where to acquire a problem-free pet, but, again, a reputable breeder is your best bet. In an ideal situation you have the opportunity to see both parents, get references from other owners of the breeder's pups and see genetic-testing documentation for several generations of the litter's ancestors. At the very least, you must thoroughly investigate the Bedlington Terrier and the problems inherent in that breed, as well as the genetic testing available to screen for those problems. Genetic testing offers some important benefits but is available for only a few disorders in a relatively small number of breeds and is not available for some of the most common genetic diseases, such as hip dysplasia, cataracts, epilepsy, cardiomyopathy, etc. This area of research is indeed exciting and increasingly important, and advances will continue to be made each year. In fact, recent research has shown that there is an equivalent dog gene for 75% of known human genes, so research done in either species is likely to benefit the other.

We've also discussed that evaluating the behavioral nature of

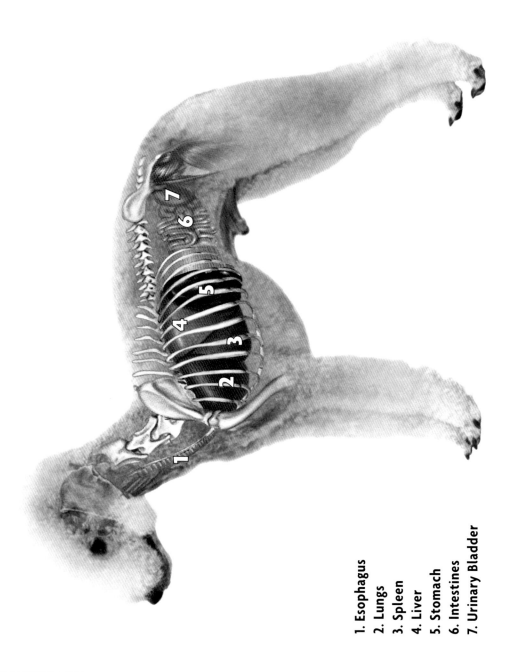

1. Esophagus
2. Lungs
3. Spleen
4. Liver
5. Stomach
6. Intestines
7. Urinary Bladder

INTERNAL ORGANS OF THE BEDLINGTON TERRIER

your Bedlington Terrier and that of his immediate family members is an important part of the selection process that cannot be overemphasized. It is sometimes difficult to evaluate temperament in puppies because certain behavioral tendencies, such as some forms of aggression, may not be immediately evident. More dogs are euthanized each year for behavioral reasons than for all medical conditions combined, so it is critical to take temperament issues seriously. Start with a well-balanced, friendly companion and put the time and effort into proper socialization, and you will be rewarded with a valued relationship for the life of the dog.

Assuming that you have started off with a pup from healthy, sound stock, you then become responsible for helping your veterinarian keep your pet healthy. Some crucial things happen before you even bring your puppy home. Parasite control typically begins at two weeks of age, and vaccinations typically begin at six to eight weeks of age. A pre-pubertal evaluation is typically scheduled for about six months of age. At this time, a dental evaluation is done (since the adult teeth are now in), heartworm prevention is started and neutering or spaying is most commonly done.

It is critical to commence regular dental care at home if you

YOUR DOG NEEDS TO VISIT THE VET IF:

- He has ingested a toxin such as antifreeze or a toxic plant; in these cases, administer first aid and call the vet right away
- His teeth are discolored, loose or missing or he has sores or other signs of infection or abnormality in the mouth
- He has been vomiting, has had diarrhea or has been constipated for over 24 hours; call immediately if you notice blood
- He has refused food for over 24 hours
- His eating habits, water intake or toilet habits have noticeably changed; if you have noticed weight gain or weight loss
- He shows symptoms of bloat, which requires *immediate* attention
- He is salivating excessively
- He has a lump in his throat
- He has a lump or bumps anywhere on the body
- He is very lethargic
- He appears to be in pain or otherwise has trouble chewing or swallowing
- His skin loses elasticity

Of course, there will be other instances in which a visit to the vet is necessary; these are just some of the signs that could be indicative of serious problems that need to be caught as early as possible.

have not already done so. It may not sound very important, but most dogs have active periodontal

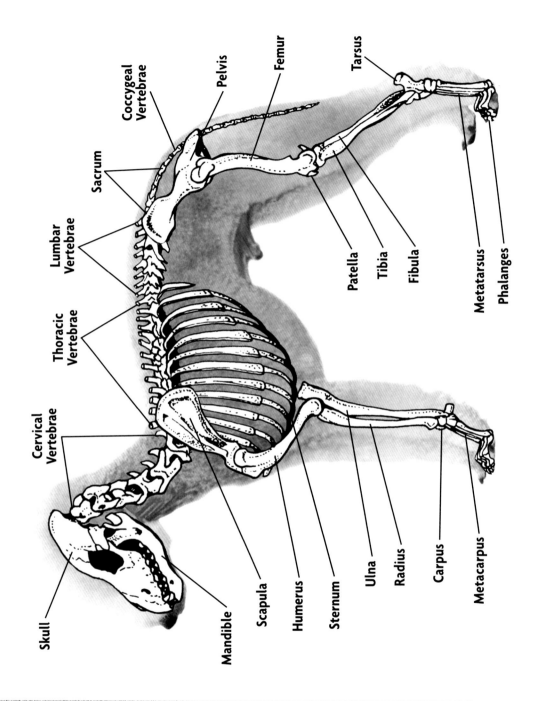

Coccygeal Vertebrae

Pelvis

Femur

Tarsus

Sacrum

Lumbar Vertebrae

Patella

Tibia

Fibula

Metatarsus

Phalanges

Thoracic Vertebrae

Cervical Vertebrae

Skull

Mandible

Scapula

Humerus

Sternum

Ulna

Radius

Carpus

Metacarpus

SKELETAL STRUCTURE OF THE BEDLINGTON TERRIER

disease by four years of age if they don't have their teeth cleaned regularly at home, not just at their veterinary exams. Dental problems lead to more than just bad "doggy breath." Gum disease can have very serious medical consequences. If you start brushing your dog's teeth and using antiseptic rinses from a young age, your dog will be accustomed to it and will not resist. The results will be healthy dentition, which

TAKING YOUR DOG'S TEMPERATURE

It is important to know how to take your dog's temperature at times when you think he may be ill. It's not the most enjoyable task, but it can be done without too much difficulty. It's easier with a helper, preferably someone with whom the dog is friendly, so that one of you can hold the dog while the other inserts the thermometer.

Before inserting the thermometer, coat the end with petroleum jelly. Insert the thermometer slowly and gently into the dog's rectum about one inch. Wait for the reading, about two minutes. Be sure to remove the thermometer carefully and clean it thoroughly after each use.

A dog's normal body temperature is between 100.5 and 102.5 degrees F. Immediate veterinary attention is required if the dog's temperature is below 99 or above 104 degrees F.

your pet will need to enjoy a long, healthy life.

Most dogs are considered adults at a year of age, although some larger breeds still have some filling out to do up to about two or so years old. Even individual dogs within each breed have different healthcare requirements, so work with your veterinarian to determine what will be needed and what your role should be. This doctor-client relationship is important, because as vaccination guidelines change, there may not be an annual "vaccine visit" scheduled. You must make sure that you see your veterinarian at least annually, even if no vaccines are due, because this is the best opportunity to coordinate healthcare activities and to make sure that no medical issues creep by unaddressed.

When your Bedlington Terrier reaches three-quarters of his anticipated lifespan, he is considered a "senior" and should start a preven-

The most important aspect of maintaining a healthy, good-looking dog is the selection of a qualified veterinarian. Here's a healthy Bedlington strutting his stuff.

PROBLEM: AND THAT STARTS WITH "P"

Urinary tract problems more commonly affect female dogs, especially those who have been spayed. The first sign that a urinary tract problem exists usually is a strong odor from the urine or an unusual color. Blood in the urine, known as hematuria, is another sign of an infection, related to cystitis, a bladder infection, bladder cancer or a blood-clotting disorder. Urinary tract problems can also be signaled by the dog's straining while urinating, experiencing pain during urination and genital discharge as well as excessive water intake and urination.

Excessive drinking, in and of itself, does not indicate a urinary tract problem. A dog who is drinking more than normal may have a kidney or liver problem, a hormonal disorder or diabetes mellitus. Behaviorists report a disorder known as psychogenic polydipsia, which manifests itself in excessive drinking and urination. If you notice your dog drinking much more than normal, take him to the vet.

tive senior-care program. In general, if you've been taking great care of your canine companion throughout his formative and adult years, the transition to senior status should be a smooth one. Age is not a disease, and as long as everything is functioning as it should, there is no reason why most of late adulthood should not be rewarding for both you and your pet. This is especially true if you have tended to the details, such as regular veterinary visits, proper dental care, excellent nutrition and management of bone and joint issues.

At the senior stage in your Bedlington Terrier's life, your veterinarian will likely schedule visits twice yearly, instead of once, to run some laboratory screenings, electrocardiograms and the like, and to change the diet to something more digestible. Catching problems early is the best way to manage them effectively. Treating the early stages of heart disease is so much easier than trying to intervene when there is more significant damage to the heart muscle. Similarly, managing the beginning of kidney problems is fairly routine if there is no significant kidney damage. Other problems, like cognitive dysfunction (similar to senility and Alzheimer's disease), cancer, diabetes and arthritis, are more common in older dogs, but all can be treated to help the dog live as many happy, comfortable years as possible. Just as in people, medical management is more effective (and less expensive) when you catch things early.

SELECTING A VETERINARIAN

There is probably no more important decision that you will make regarding your pet's healthcare than the selection of his doctor. Your pet's veterinarian will be a pediatrician, family-practice physician and gerontologist, depending on the dog's life stage, and will be the individual who makes recommendations regarding issues such as when specialists need to be consulted, when diagnostic testing and/or therapeutic intervention is needed and when you will need to seek outside emergency and critical-care services. Your vet will act as your advocate and liaison throughout these processes.

Everyone has his own idea about what to look for in a vet, an individual who will play a big role in his dog's (and, of course, his own) life for many years to come. For some, it is the compassionate caregiver with whom they hope to develop a professional relationship to span the lives of their dogs and even their future pets. For others, they are seeking a clinician with keen diagnostic and therapeutic insight who can deliver state-of-the-art healthcare. Still others need a veterinary facility that is open evenings and weekends, is in close proximity or provides mobile veterinary services to accommodate their schedules; these people may not much mind that their dogs might see different veterinarians on each visit. Just as we have different reasons for selecting our own

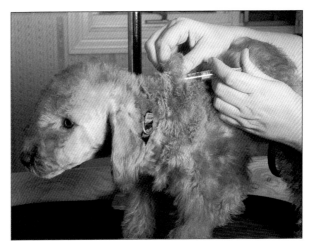

Vaccinations are an important component of keeping your Bedlington free from disease.

healthcare professionals (e.g., covered by insurance plan, expert in field, convenient location, etc.), we should not expect that there is a one-size-fits-all recommendation for selecting a veterinarian and veterinary practice. The best advice is to be honest in your assessment of what you expect from a veterinary practice and to conscientiously research the options in your area. You will quickly appreciate that not all veterinary practices are the same, and you will be happiest with one that truly meets your needs.

There is another point to be considered in the selection of veterinary services. Not that long ago, a single veterinarian would attempt to manage all medical and surgical issues as they arose. That was often problematic, because veterinarians are trained in many species and many diseases, and it was just impossible for general

HEARTWORM ZONE

Although heartworm cases have been reported in all 48 continental states, the largest threat exists in the Southeast and Mississippi River Valley. The following states have the highest risk factors: Texas, Florida, Louisiana, North Carolina, Georgia, Mississippi, Tennessee, South Carolina, Alabama and Indiana. Discuss the risk factor with your veterinarian to determine your course of prevention for your dog.

veterinary practitioners to be experts in every species, every breed, every field and every ailment. However, just as in the human healthcare fields, specialization has allowed general practitioners to concentrate on primary healthcare delivery, especially wellness and the prevention of infectious diseases, and to utilize a network of specialists to assist in the management of conditions that require specific expertise and experience. Thus there are now many types of veterinary specialists, including dermatologists, cardiologists, ophthalmologists, surgeons, internists, oncologists, neurologists, behaviorists, criticalists and others to help primary-care veterinarians deal with complicated medical challenges. In most cases, specialists see cases referred by primary-care veterinarians, make diagnoses and set up

management plans. From there, the animals' ongoing care is returned to their primary-care veterinarians. This important team approach to your pet's medical-care needs has provided opportunities for advanced care and an unparalleled level of quality to be delivered.

With all of the opportunities for your Bedlington Terrier to receive high-quality veterinary medical care, there is another topic that needs to be addressed at the same time—cost. It's been said that you can have excellent healthcare or inexpensive healthcare, but never both; this is as true in veterinary medicine as it is in human medicine. While veterinary costs are a fraction of what the same services cost in the human healthcare arena, it is still difficult to deal with unanticipated medical costs, especially since they can easily creep into hundreds or even thousands of dollars if specialists or emergency services become involved. However, there are ways of managing these risks. The easiest is to buy pet health insurance and realize that its foremost purpose is not to cover routine healthcare visits but rather to serve as an umbrella for those rainy days when your pet needs medical care and you don't want to worry about whether or not you can afford that care.

Pet insurance policies are very cost-effective (and very inexpensive by human health-insurance standards), but make sure that you buy the policy long before you intend to use it (preferably starting in puppyhood, because coverage will exclude pre-existing conditions) and that you are actually buying an indemnity insurance plan from an insurance company that is regulated by your state or province. Many insurance policy look-alikes are actually discount clubs that are redeemable only at specific locations and for specific services. An indemnity plan covers your pet at almost all veterinary, specialty and emergency practices and is an excellent way to manage your pet's ongoing healthcare needs.

VACCINATIONS AND INFECTIOUS DISEASES

There has never been an easier time to prevent a variety of infectious diseases in your dog, but the advances we've made in veterinary medicine come with a price—choice. Now while this choice is a good thing, it also has never been more difficult for the pet owner (or the veterinarian) to make an informed decision about the best way to protect pets through vaccination.

Years ago, it was just accepted that puppies got a starter series of vaccinations and then annual "boosters" throughout their lives to keep them protected. As more and more vaccines became avail-

able, consumers wanted the convenience of having all of that protection in a single injection. The result was "multivalent" vaccines that crammed a lot of protection into a single syringe. The manufacturers' recommendations were to give the vaccines annually, and this was a simple enough protocol to follow. However, as veterinary medicine has become more sophisticated

DENTAL WARNING SIGNS
A veterinary dental exam is necessary if you notice one or any combination of the following in your dog:
- Broken, loose or missing teeth
- Loss of appetite (which could be due to mouth pain or illness caused by infection)
- Gum abnormalities, including redness, swelling and bleeding
- Drooling, with or without blood
- Yellowing of the teeth or gumline, indicating tartar
- Bad breath

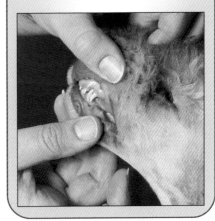

COMMON INFECTIOUS DISEASES

Let's discuss some of the diseases that create the need for vaccination in the first place. Following are the major canine infectious diseases and a simple explanation of each.

Rabies: A devastating viral disease that can be fatal in dogs and people. In fact, vaccination of dogs and cats is an important public-health measure to create a resistant animal buffer population to protect people from contracting the disease. Vaccination schedules are determined on a government level and are not optional for pet owners; rabies vaccination is required by law in all 50 states.

Parvovirus: A severe, potentially life-threatening disease that is easily transmitted between dogs. There are four strains of the virus, but it is believed that there is significant "cross-protection" between strains that may be included in individual vaccines.

Distemper: A potentially severe and life-threatening disease with a relatively high risk of exposure, especially in certain regions. In very high-risk distemper environments, young pups may be vaccinated with human measles vaccine, a related virus that offers cross-protection when administered at four to ten weeks of age.

Hepatitis: Caused by canine adenovirus type 1 (CAV-1), but since vaccination with the causative virus has a higher rate of adverse effects, cross-protection is derived from the use of adenovirus type 2 (CAV-2), a cause of respiratory disease and one of the potential causes of canine cough. Vaccination with CAV-2 provides long-term immunity against hepatitis, but relatively less protection against respiratory infection.

Canine cough: Also called tracheobronchitis, actually a fairly complicated result of viral and bacterial offenders; therefore, even with vaccination, protection is incomplete. Wherever dogs congregate, canine cough will likely be spread among them. Intranasal vaccination with *Bordetella* and parainfluenza is the best safeguard, but the duration of immunity does not appear to be very long, typically a year at most. These are non-core vaccines, but vaccination is sometimes mandated by boarding kennels, obedience classes, dog shows and other places where dogs congregate to try to minimize spread of infection.

Leptospirosis: A potentially fatal disease that is more common in some geographic regions. It is capable of being spread to humans. The disease varies with the individual "serovar," or strain, of *Leptospira* involved. Since there does not appear to be much cross-protection between serovars, protection is only as good as the likelihood that the serovar in the vaccine is the same as the one in the pet's local environment. Problems with *Leptospira* vaccines are that protection does not last very long, side effects are not uncommon and a large percentage of dogs (perhaps 30%) may not respond to vaccination.

Borrelia burgdorferi: The cause of Lyme disease, the risk of which varies with the geographic area in which the pet lives and travels. Lyme disease is spread by deer ticks in the eastern US and western black-legged ticks in the western part of the country, and the risk of exposure is high in some regions. Lameness, fever and inappetence are most commonly seen in affected dogs. The extent of protection from the vaccine has not been conclusively demonstrated.

Coronavirus: This disease has a high risk of exposure, especially in areas where dogs congregate, but it typically causes only mild to moderate digestive upset (diarrhea, vomiting, etc.). Vaccines are available, but the duration of protection is believed to be relatively short and the effectiveness of the vaccine in preventing infection is considered low.

There are many other vaccinations available, including those for *Giardia* and canine adenovirus-1. While there may be some specific indications for their use, and local risk factors to be considered, they are not widely recommended for most dogs.

and we have started looking more at healthcare quandaries rather than convenience, it became necessary to reevaluate the situation and deal with some tough questions. It is important to realize that whether or not to use a particular vaccine depends on the risk of contracting the disease against which it protects, the severity of the disease if it is contracted, the duration of immunity provided by the vaccine, the safety of the product and the needs of the individual animal. In a very general sense, rabies, distemper, hepatitis and parvovirus are considered core vaccine needs, while parainfluenza, *Bordetella bronchiseptica*, leptospirosis, coronavirus and borreliosis (Lyme disease) are considered non-core needs and best reserved for animals that demonstrate reasonable risk of contracting the diseases.

NEUTERING/SPAYING

Sterilization procedures (neutering for males/spaying for females) are meant to accomplish several purposes. While the underlying premise is to address the risk of pet overpopulation, there are also some medical and behavioral benefits to the surgeries. For females, spaying prior to the first estrus (heat cycle) leads to a marked reduction in the risk of mammary cancer and other serious female problems. There also will be no manifestations of "heat" to attract male dogs and no bleeding in the house. For males, there is prevention of testicular cancer and a reduction in the risk of prostate problems. In both sexes there may be some limited reduction in aggressive behaviors toward other dogs, and some diminishing of urine marking, roaming and mounting.

In females, spaying is specifically referred to as an ovariohysterectomy. In this procedure, a midline incision is made in the abdomen and the entire uterus and both ovaries are surgically removed. In males, neutering has traditionally referred to castration, which involves the surgical removal of both testicles. In addition, there is now a chemical sterilization option. This is a relatively new approach, and there are no long-term clinical studies yet available.

Neutering/spaying is typically done around six months of age at most veterinary hospitals, although techniques have been pioneered to perform the procedures in animals as young as eight weeks of age. In general, the surgeries on the very young animals are done for the specific reason of sterilizing them before they go to their new homes. This is done in some shelter hospitals for assurance that the animals will definitely not produce any pups.

A scanning electron micrograph of a dog flea, Ctenocephalides canis, on dog hair.

EXTERNAL PARASITES

FLEAS

Fleas have been around for millions of years and, while we have better tools now for controlling them than at any time in the past, there still is little chance that they will end up on an endangered species list. Actually, they are very well adapted to living on our pets, and they continue to adapt as we make advances.

The female flea can consume 15 times her weight in blood during active reproduction and can lay as many as 40 eggs a day. These eggs are very resistant to the effects of insecticides. They hatch into larvae, which then mature and spin cocoons. The immature fleas reside in this pupal stage until the time is right for feeding. This pupal stage is also very resistant to the effects of insecticides, and pupae can last in the environment without feeding for many months. Newly emergent fleas are attracted to animals by the warmth of the animals' bodies, movement and exhaled carbon dioxide. However, when they first emerge from their cocoons, they orient towards light; thus when an animal passes between a flea and the light source, casting a shadow, the flea pounces and starts to feed. If the animal turns out to be a dog or cat, the reproductive cycle continues. If the flea lands on another type of animal, including a person, the flea will bite but will then look for a more appropriate host. An emerging adult flea can survive without feeding for up to 12 months but, once it tastes blood, it can survive off its host for only 3 to 4 days.

It was once thought that fleas spend most of their lives in the environment, but we now know that fleas won't willingly jump off a dog unless leaping to another dog or when physically removed by brushing, bathing or other manipulation. Flea eggs, on the other hand, are shiny and smooth, and they roll off the animal and into the environment. The eggs, larvae and pupae then exist in the environment, but once the adult finds a susceptible animal, it's home sweet home until the flea is forced to seek refuge elsewhere.

Since adult fleas live on the animal and immature forms survive in the environment, a successful treatment plan must address all stages of the flea life cycle. There are now several safe and effective flea-control products that can be applied on a monthly

> ### FLEA PREVENTION FOR YOUR DOG
> - Discuss with your veterinarian the safest product to protect your dog, likely in the form of a monthly tablet or a liquid preparation placed on the back of the dog's neck.
> - For dogs suffering from flea-bite dermatitis, a shampoo or topical insecticide treatment is required.
> - Your lawn and property should be sprayed with an insecticide designed to kill fleas and ticks that lurk outdoors.
> - Using a flea comb, check the dog's coat regularly for any signs of parasites.
> - Practice good housekeeping. Vacuum floors, carpets and furniture regularly, especially in the areas that the dog frequents, and wash the dog's bedding weekly.
> - Follow up house-cleaning with carpet shampoos and sprays to rid the house of fleas at all stages of development. Insect growth regulators are the safest option.

basis. These include fipronil, imidacloprid, selamectin and permethrin (found in several formulations). Most of these products have significant flea-killing rates within 24 hours. However, none of them will control the immature forms in the environment. To accomplish this, there are a variety of insect growth regulators that can be sprayed into

THE FLEA'S LIFE CYCLE

What came first, the flea or the egg? This age-old mystery is more difficult to comprehend than the actual cycle of the flea. Fleas usually live only about four months. A female can lay 2,000 eggs in her lifetime.

Egg

After ten days of rolling around your carpet or under your furniture, the eggs hatch into larvae, which feed on various and sundry debris. In days or

Larva

months, depending on the climate, the larvae spin cocoons and develop into the pupal or nymph stage, which quickly develop into fleas.

Pupa

These immature fleas must locate a host within 10 to 14 days or they will die. Only about 1% of the flea population exist as adult fleas, while the other 99% exist as eggs, larvae or pupae.

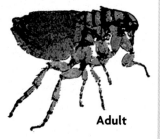

Adult

KILL FLEAS THE NATURAL WAY

If you choose not to go the route of conventional medication, there are some natural ways to ward off fleas:

- Dust your dog with a natural flea powder, composed of such herbal goodies as rosemary, wormwood, pennyroyal, citronella, rue, tobacco powder and eucalyptus.
- Apply diatomaceous earth, the fossilized remains of single-cell algae, to your carpets, furniture and pet's bedding. Even though it's not good for dogs, it's even worse for fleas, which will dry up swiftly and die.
- Brush your dog frequently, give him adequate exercise and let him fast occasionally. All of these activities strengthen the dog's immune system and make him more resistant to disease and parasites.
- Bathe your dog with a capful of pennyroyal or eucalyptus oil.
- Feed a natural diet, free of additives and preservatives. Add some fresh garlic and brewer's yeast to the dog's morning portion, as these items have flea-repelling properties.

the environment (e.g., pyriprox-yfen, methoprene, fenoxycarb) as well as insect development inhibitors such as lufenuron that can be administered. These compounds have no effect on adult fleas, but they stop imma-ture forms from developing into adults. In years gone by, we relied heavily on toxic insecticides (such as organophosphates, organochlo-rines and carbamates) to manage the flea problem, but today's options are not only much safer to use on our pets but also safer for the environment.

Photo by Carolina Biological Supply Co.

TICKS

Ticks are members of the spider class (arachnids) and are blood-sucking parasites capable of transmitting a variety of diseases, including Lyme disease, ehrlichiosis, babesiosis and Rocky Mountain spotted fever. It's easy to see ticks on your own skin, but it is more of a challenge when your furry companion is affected. Whenever you happen to be planning a stroll in a tick-infested area (especially forests, grassy or wooded areas or parks) be prepared to do a thorough inspection of your dog afterward to search for ticks. Ticks can be tricky, so make sure you spend time looking in the ears, between the toes and everywhere else where a tick might hide. Ticks need to be attached for 24–72 hours before they transmit most of the diseases that they carry, so you do have a window of opportunity for some preventive intervention.

A TICKING BOMB

There is nothing good about a tick's harpooning his nose into your dog's skin. Among the diseases caused by ticks are Rocky Mountain spotted fever, canine ehrlichiosis, canine babesiosis, canine hepatozoonosis and Lyme disease. If a dog is allergic to the saliva of a female wood tick, he can develop tick paralysis.

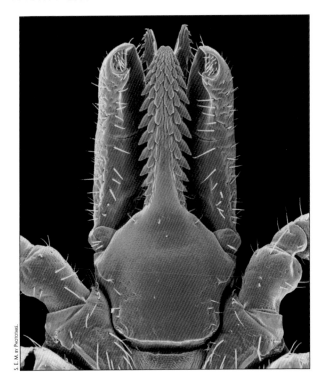

S. E. M. BY PHOTOTAKE.

A scanning electron micrograph of the head of a female deer tick, *Ixodes dammini*, a parasitic tick that carries Lyme disease.

Female ticks live to eat and breed. They can lay between 4,000 and 5,000 eggs and they die soon after. Males, on the other hand, live only to mate with the females and continue the process as long as they are able. Most ticks live on multiple hosts before parasitizing dogs. The immature forms typically reside on grass and shrubs, waiting for susceptible animals to walk by. The larvae and nymph stages typically feed on wildlife.

If only a few ticks are present on a dog, they can be plucked out, but it is important to remove the entire head and mouthparts,

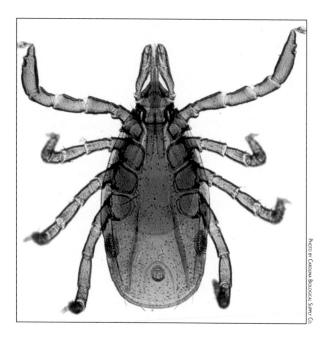

PHOTO BY CAROLINA BIOLOGICAL SUPPLY CO.

Deer tick,
Ixodes dammini.

of in a container of alcohol or household bleach.

Some of the newer flea products, specifically those with fipronil, selamectin and permethrin, have effect against some, but not all, species of tick. Flea collars containing appropriate pesticides (e.g., propoxur, chlorfenvinphos) can aid in tick control. In most areas, such collars should be placed on animals in March, at the beginning of the tick season, and changed regularly. Leaving the collar on when the pesticide level is waning invites the development of resistance. Amitraz collars are also good for tick control, and the active ingredient does not interfere with other flea-control products. The ingredient helps prevent the attachment of ticks to the skin and will cause those ticks already on the skin to detach themselves.

which may be deeply embedded in the skin. This is best accomplished with forceps designed especially for this purpose; fingers can be used but should be protected with rubber gloves, plastic wrap or at least a paper towel. The tick should be grasped as closely as possible to the animal's skin and should be pulled upward with steady, even pressure. Do not squeeze, crush or puncture the body of the tick or you risk exposure to any disease carried by that tick. Once the ticks have been removed, the sites of attachment should be disinfected. Your hands should then be washed with soap and water to further minimize risk of contagion. The tick should be disposed

TICK CONTROL

Removal of underbrush and leaf litter and the thinning of trees in areas where tick control is desired are recommended. These actions remove the cover and food sources for small animals that serve as hosts for ticks. With continued mowing of grasses in these areas, the probability of ticks' surviving is further reduced. A variety of insecticide ingredients (e.g., resmethrin, carbaryl, permethrin, chlorpyrifos, dioxathion and allethrin) are registered for tick control around the home.

MITES

Mites are tiny arachnid parasites that parasitize the skin of dogs. Skin diseases caused by mites are referred to as "mange," and there are many different forms seen in dogs. These forms are very different from one another, each one warranting an individual description.

Sarcoptic mange, or scabies, is one of the itchiest conditions that affects dogs. The microscopic *Sarcoptes* mites burrow into the superficial layers of the skin and can drive dogs crazy with itchiness. They are also communicable to people, although they can't complete their reproductive cycle on people. In addition to being tiny, the mites also are often difficult to find when trying to make a diagnosis. Skin scrapings from multiple areas are examined microscopically but, even then, sometimes the mites cannot be found.

Fortunately, scabies is relatively easy to treat, and there are a variety of products that will successfully kill the mites. Since the mites can't live in the environment for very long without feeding, a complete cure is usually possible within four to eight weeks.

Cheyletiellosis is caused by a relatively large mite, which sometimes can be seen even without a microscope. Often referred to as "walking dandruff," this also causes itching, but not usually as profound as with scabies. While *Cheyletiella* mites can survive somewhat longer

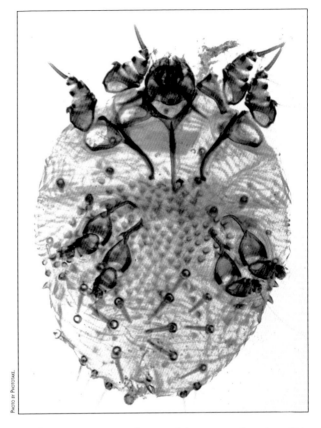

PHOTO BY PHOTOTAKE.

Sarcoptes scabiei, commonly known as the "itch mite."

in the environment than scabies mites, they too are relatively easy to treat, being responsive to not only the medications used to treat scabies but also often to flea-control products.

Otodectes cynotis is the canine ear mite and is one of the more common causes of mange, especially in young dogs in shelters or pet stores. That's because the mites are typically present in large numbers and are quickly spread to nearby animals. The mites rarely do much harm but can be difficult

Micrograph of a dog louse, *Heterodoxus spiniger*. Female lice attach their eggs to the hairs of the dog. As the eggs hatch, the larval lice bite and feed on the blood. Lice can also feed on dead skin and hair. This feeding activity can cause hair loss and skin problems.

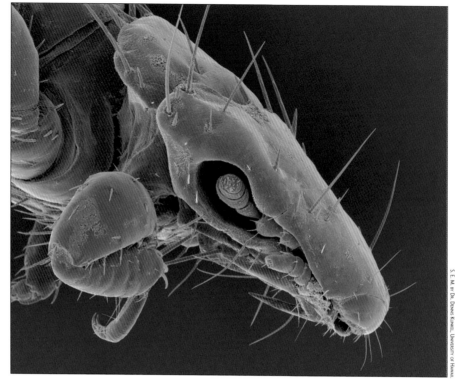

S.E.M. BY DR. DENNIS KUNKEL, UNIVERSITY OF HAWAII.

to eradicate if the treatment regimen is not comprehensive. While many try to treat the condition with ear drops only, this is the most common cause of treatment failure. Ear drops cause the mites to simply move out of the ears and as far away as possible (usually to the base of the tail) until the insecticide levels in the ears drop to an acceptable level—then it's back to business as usual! The successful treatment of ear mites requires treating all animals in the household with a systemic insecticide, such as selamectin, or a combination of miticidal ear drops

combined with whole-body flea-control preparations.

Demodicosis, sometimes referred to as red mange, can be one of the most difficult forms of mange to treat. Part of the problem has to do with the fact that the mites live in the hair follicles and they are relatively well shielded from topical and systemic products. The main issue, however, is that demodectic mange typically results only when there is some underlying process interfering with the dog's immune system.

Since *Demodex* mites are normal residents of the skin of

mammals, including humans, there is usually a mite population explosion only when the immune system fails to keep the number of mites in check. In young animals, the immune deficit may be transient or may reflect an actual inherited immune problem. In older animals, demodicosis is usually seen only when there is another disease hampering the immune system, such as diabetes, cancer, thyroid problems or the use of immune-suppressing drugs. Accordingly, treatment involves not only trying to kill the mange mites but also discerning what is interfering with immune function and correcting it if possible.

Chiggers represent several different species of mite that don't parasitize dogs specifically, but do latch on to passersby and can cause irritation. The problem is most prevalent in wooded areas in the late summer and fall. Treatment is not difficult, as the mites do not complete their life cycle on dogs and are susceptible to a variety of miticidal products.

MOSQUITOES

Mosquitoes have long been known to transmit a variety of diseases to people, as well as just being biting pests during warm weather. They also pose a real risk to pets. Not only do they carry deadly heartworms but

Illustration of *Demodex folliculoram.*

recently there also has been much concern over their involvement with West Nile virus. While we can avoid heartworm with the use of preventive medications, there are no such preventives for West Nile virus. The only method of prevention in endemic areas is active mosquito control. Fortunately, most dogs that have been exposed to the virus only developed flu-like symptoms and, to date, there have not been the large number of reported deaths in canines as seen in some other species.

MOSQUITO REPELLENT

Low concentrations of DEET (less than 10%), found in many human mosquito repellents, have been safely used on dogs but, in these concentrations, probably give only about two hours of protection. DEET may be safe in these small concentrations, but since it is not licensed for use on dogs, there is no research proving its safety for dogs. Products containing permethrin give the longest-lasting protection, perhaps two to four weeks. As DEET is not licensed for use on dogs, and both DEET and permethrin can be quite toxic to cats, appropriate care should be exercised. Other products, such as those containing oil of citronella, also have some mosquito-repellent activity, but typically have a relatively short duration of action.

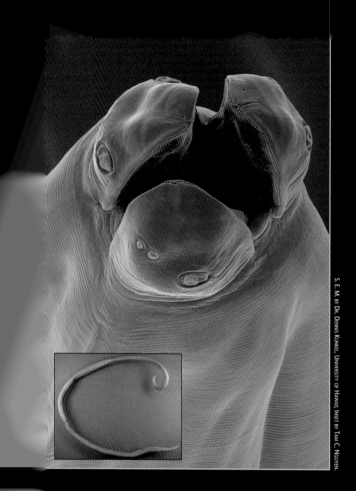

S. E. M. BY DR. DENNIS KUNKEL, UNIVERSITY OF HAWAII. INSET BY TAM C. NGUYEN.

The ascarid roundworm *Toxocara canis*, showing the mouth with three lips. INSET: photomicrograph of the roundworm *Ascaris lumbricoides*.

INTERNAL PARASITES: WORMS

ASCARIDS

Ascarids are intestinal round-worms that rarely cause severe disease in dogs. Nonetheless, they are of major public health significance because they can be transferred to people. Sadly, it is children who are most commonly affected by the parasite, probably from inadvertently ingesting ascarid-contaminated soil. In fact, many yards and children's sand-boxes contain appreciable numbers of ascarid eggs. So, while ascarids don't bite dogs or latch onto their intestines to suck blood, they do cause some nasty medical conditions in children and are best eradicated from our furry friends. Because pups can start passing ascarid eggs by three weeks of age, most parasite-control programs begin at two weeks of age and are repeated every two weeks until pups are eight weeks old. It is important to

HOOKED ON ANCYLOSTOMA

Adult dogs can become infected by the bloodsucking nematodes we commonly call hookworms via ingesting larvae from the ground or via the larvae penetrating the dog's skin. It is not uncommon for infected dogs to show no symptoms of hookworm infestation. Sometimes symptoms occur within ten days of exposure. These symptoms can include bloody diarrhea, anemia, loss of weight and general weakness. Dogs pass the hookworm eggs in their stools, which serves as the vet's method of identifying the infestation. The hookworm larvae can encyst themselves in the dog's tissues and be released when the dog is experiencing stress.

Caused by an *Ancylostoma* species whose common host is the dog, cutaneous larval migrans affects humans, causing itching and lumps and streaks beneath the surface of the skin.

S. E. M. by Dr. Dennis Kunkel, University of Hawaii.

realize that bitches can pass ascarids to their pups even if they test negative prior to whelping. Accordingly, bitches are best treated at the same time as the pups.

HOOKWORMS

Unlike ascarids, hookworms do latch onto a dog's intestinal tract and can cause significant loss of blood and protein. Similar to ascarids, hookworms can be transmitted to humans, where they cause a condition known as cutaneous larval migrans. Dogs can become infected either by consuming the infective larvae or by the larvae's penetrating the skin directly. People most often get infected when they are lying on the ground (such as on a beach) and the larvae penetrate the skin. Yes, the larvae can penetrate through a beach blanket. Hookworms are typically susceptible to the same medications used to treat ascarids.

The hookworm *Ancylostoma caninum* infests the intestines of dogs. INSET: Note the row of hooks at the posterior end, used to anchor the worm to the intestinal wall.

WHIPWORMS

Whipworms latch onto the lower aspects of the dog's colon and can cause cramping and diarrhea. Eggs do not start to appear in the dog's feces until about three months after the dog was infected. This worm has a peculiar life cycle, which makes it more difficult to control than ascarids or hookworms. The good thing is that whipworms rarely are transferred to people.

Some of the medications used to treat ascarids and hookworms are also effective against whipworms, but, in general, a separate treatment protocol is needed. Since most of the medications are effective against the adults but not the eggs or larvae, treatment is typically repeated in three weeks, and then often in three

WORM-CONTROL GUIDELINES

- Practice sanitary habits with your dog and home.
- Clean up after your dog and don't let him sniff or eat other dogs' droppings.
- Control insects and fleas in the dog's environment. Fleas, lice, cockroaches, beetles, mice and rats can act as hosts for various worms.
- Prevent dogs from eating uncooked meat, raw poultry and dead animals.
- Keep dogs and children from playing in sand and soil.
- Kennel dogs on cement or gravel; avoid dirt runs.
- Administer heartworm preventives regularly.
- Have your vet examine your dog's stools at your annual visits.
- Select a boarding kennel carefully so as to avoid contamination from other dogs or an unsanitary environment.
- Prevent dogs from roaming. Obey local leash laws.

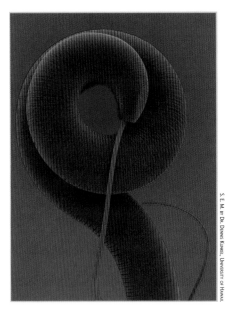

Adult whipworm, *Trichuris* sp., an intestinal parasite.

S. E. M. BY DR. DENNIS KUNKEL, UNIVERSITY OF HAWAII

months as well. Unfortunately, since dogs don't develop resistance to whipworms, it is difficult to prevent them from getting reinfected if they visit soil contaminated with whipworm eggs.

TAPEWORMS

There are many different species of tapeworm that affect dogs, but *Dipylidium caninum* is probably the most common and is spread by fleas. Flea larvae feed on organic debris and tapeworm eggs in the environment and, when a dog chews at himself and manages to ingest fleas, he might get a dose of tapeworm at the same time. The tapeworm then develops further in the intestine of the dog.

The tapeworm itself, which is a parasitic flatworm that latches onto the intestinal wall, is composed of numerous segments. When the segments break off into the intestine (as proglottids), they may accumulate around the rectum, like grains of rice. While this tapeworm is disgusting in its behavior, it is not directly communicable to humans (although humans can also get infected by swallowing fleas).

A much more dangerous flatworm is *Echinococcus multilocularis*, which is typically found in foxes, coyotes and wolves. The eggs are passed in the feces and infect rodents, and, when dogs eat the rodents, the dogs can be infected by thousands of adult tapeworms. While the parasites don't cause many problems in dogs, this is considered the most lethal worm infection that people can get. Take appropriate precautions if you live in an area in which these tapeworms are found. Do not use mulch that may contain feces of dogs, cats or wildlife, and discourage your pets from hunting

wildlife. Treat these tapeworm infections aggressively in pets, because if humans get infected, approximately half die.

HEARTWORMS

Heartworm disease is caused by the parasite *Dirofilaria immitis* and is seen in dogs around the world. A member of the roundworm group, it is spread between dogs by the bite of an infected mosquito. The mosquito injects infective larvae into the dog's skin with its bite, and these larvae develop under the skin for a period of time before making their way to the heart. There they develop into adults, which grow and create blockages of the heart, lungs and major blood vessels there. They also start producing offspring (microfilariae),

A dog tapeworm proglottid (body segment).

The dog tapeworm *Taenia pisiformis.*

S. E. M. BY DR. DENNIS KUNKEL, UNIVERSITY OF HAWAII.

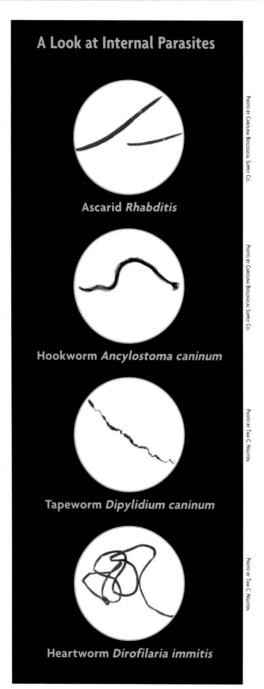

A Look at Internal Parasites

Ascarid *Rhabditis*

Hookworm *Ancylostoma caninum*

Tapeworm *Dipylidium caninum*

Heartworm *Dirofilaria immitis*

and these microfilariae circulate in the bloodstream, waiting to hitch a ride when the next mosquito bites. Once in the mosquito, the microfilariae develop into infective larvae and the entire process is repeated.

When dogs get infected with heartworm, over time they tend to develop symptoms associated with heart disease, such as coughing, exercise intolerance and potentially many other manifestations. Diagnosis is confirmed by either seeing the microfilariae themselves in blood samples or using immunologic tests (antigen testing) to identify the presence of adult heartworms. Since antigen tests measure the presence of adult heartworms and microfilarial tests measure offspring produced by adults, neither are positive until six to seven months after the initial infection. However, the beginning of damage can occur by fifth-stage larvae as early as three months after infection. Thus it is possible for dogs to be harboring problem-causing larvae for up to three months before either type of test would identify an infection.

The good news is that there are great protocols available for preventing heartworm in dogs. Testing is critical in the process, and it is important to understand the benefits as well as the limitations of such testing. All dogs six months of age or older that have not been on continuous heartworm-preventive medication should be

Life Cycle of the Heartworm

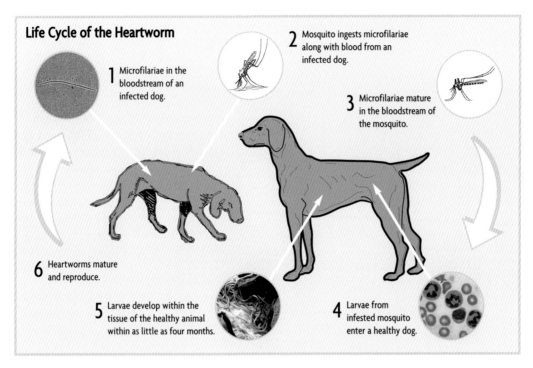

1 Microfilariae in the bloodstream of an infected dog.

2 Mosquito ingests microfilariae along with blood from an infected dog.

3 Microfilariae mature in the bloodstream of the mosquito.

4 Larvae from infested mosquito enter a healthy dog.

5 Larvae develop within the tissue of the healthy animal within as little as four months.

6 Heartworms mature and reproduce.

screened with microfilarial or antigen tests. For dogs receiving preventive medication, periodic antigen testing helps assess the effectiveness of the preventives. The American Heartworm Society guidelines suggest that annual retesting may not be necessary when owners have absolutely provided continuous heartworm prevention. Retesting on a two- to three-year interval may be sufficient in these cases. However, your veterinarian will likely have specific guidelines under which heartworm preventives will be prescribed, and many prefer to err on the side of safety and retest annually.

It is indeed fortunate that heartworm is relatively easy to prevent, because treatments can be as life-threatening as the disease itself. Treatment requires a two-step process that kills the adult heartworms first and then the microfilariae. Prevention is obviously preferable; this involves a once-monthly oral or topical treatment. The most common oral preventives include ivermectin (not suitable for some breeds), moxidectin and milbemycin oxime; the once-a-month topical drug selamectin provides heartworm protection in addition to flea, some types of tick and other parasite controls.

BEDLINGTON TERRIER

When we bring home a puppy, full of the energy and exuberance that accompanies youth, we hope for a long, happy and fulfilling relationship with the new family member. Even when we adopt an older dog, we look forward to the years of companionship ahead with a new canine friend. However, aging is inevitable for all creatures, and there will come a time when your Bedlington Terrier reaches his senior years and will need special considerations and attention to his care.

WHEN IS MY DOG A "SENIOR"?

In general, pure-bred dogs are considered to have achieved senior status when they reach 75% of their breed's average lifespan, with lifespan being based on size and breed-specific factors. Your Bedlington Terrier has an average lifespan of 12–14 and, using this rule, is considered a senior citizen at around age 9.

Obviously, the old "seven dog years to one human year" theory is not exact. In puppyhood, a dog's year is actually comparable to more than seven human years, considering the puppy's rapid growth during his first year. Then,

in adulthood, the ratio decreases. Regardless, the more viable rule of thumb is that the larger the dog, the shorter his expected lifespan. Of course, this can vary among individual dogs, with many living longer than expected, which we hope is the case!

WHAT ARE THE SIGNS OF AGING?

By the time your dog has reached his senior years, you will know him very well, so the physical and behavioral changes that accompany aging should be noticeable to you. Humans and dogs share the most obvious physical sign of aging: gray hair! Graying often occurs first on the muzzle and face, around the eyes. Other telltale signs are the dog's overall decrease in activity. Your older dog might be more content to nap and rest, and he may not show the same old enthusiasm when it's time to play in the yard or go for a walk. Other physical signs include significant weight loss or gain; more labored movement; skin and coat problems, possibly hair loss; sight and/or hearing problems; changes in toileting habits, perhaps seeming "unhousebroken" at times; and tooth decay, bad breath or other mouth problems.

There are behavioral changes that go along with aging, too. There are numerous causes for behavioral changes. Sometimes a dog's apparent confusion results from a physical change like diminished sight or hearing. If his confusion causes him to be afraid, he may act aggressively or defensively. He may sleep more frequently because his daily walks, though shorter now, tire him out. He may begin to experience separation anxiety or, conversely, become less interested in petting and attention.

There also are clinical conditions that cause behavioral changes in older dogs. One such condition is known as canine cognitive dysfunction (familiarly known as "old-dog" syndrome). It can be frustrating for an owner whose dog is affected with cognitive dysfunction, as it can result in behavioral changes of all types, most seemingly unexplainable. Common changes include the dog's forgetting aspects of the daily routine, such as times to eat, go out for walks, relieve himself and the like. Along the same lines, you may take your dog out at the regular time for a potty trip and he may have no idea why he is there. Sometimes a placid dog will begin to show aggressive or possessive tenden-

cies or, conversely, a hyperactive dog will start to "mellow out."

Disease also can be the cause of behavioral changes in senior dogs. Hormonal problems

AH, MY ACHING BONES!

As your pet ages and things that once were routine become difficult for him to handle, you may need to make some adjustments around the home to make things easier for your dog. Senior dogs affected by arthritis may have trouble moving about. If you notice this in your dog, you may have to limit him to one floor of the house so that he does not have to deal with stairs. If there are a few steps leading out into the yard, a ramp may help the dog. Likewise, he may need a ramp or a boost to get in and out of the car. Ensure that he has plenty of soft bedding on which to sleep and rest, as this will be comfortable for his aching joints. Also ensure that surfaces on which the dog walks are not slippery.

Investigate new dietary supplements made for arthritic dogs. Studies have found that products containing glucosamine added once or twice daily to the senior dog's food can have beneficial effects on the dog's joints. Many of these products also contain natural anti-inflammatories such as chondroitin, MSM and cetyl myristoleate, as well as natural herbal remedies and nutmeg. Talk to your vet about these supplements.

(Cushing's disease is common in older dogs), diabetes and thyroid disease can cause increased appetite, which can lead to aggression related to food guarding. It's better to be proactive with your senior dog, making more frequent trips to the vet if necessary and having bloodwork done to test for the diseases that can commonly befall older dogs.

This is not to say that, as dogs age, they all fall apart physically and become nasty in personality. The aforementioned changes are discussed to alert owners to the things that may happen as their

Old-timers may be more sensitive to heat or cold. A doggie sweater can help ward off the chill in cooler weather.

dogs get older. Many hardy dogs remain active and alert well into old age. However, it can be frustrating and heartbreaking for owners to see their beloved dogs change physically and temperamentally. Just know that it's the same Bedlington Terrier under there, and that he still loves you and appreciates your care, which he needs now more than ever.

HOW DO I CARE FOR MY AGING DOG?

Again, every dog is an individual in terms of aging. Your dog might advance in years and show no signs of slowing down. However, even if he shows no outward signs of aging, your vet will likely recommend starting a preventive senior-care program when your Bedlington reaches seven or eight years of age. He may not show it, but he's not a pup anymore! By providing him with extra attention to his veterinary care at this age, you will be practicing good preventive medicine, ensuring that the rest of your dog's life will be as long, active, happy and healthy as possible. If you do notice indications of aging, such as graying and/or changes in sleeping, eating or toileting habits, this is a sign to set up a senior-care visit with your vet right away to make sure that these changes are not related to any health problems.

To start, senior dogs should visit the vet twice yearly for

Number-One Killer Disease in Dogs: CANCER

In every age, there is a word associated with a disease or plague that causes humans to shudder. In the 21st century, that word is "cancer." Just as cancer is the leading cause of death in humans, it claims nearly half the lives of dogs that die from a natural disease as well as half the dogs that die over the age of ten years.

Described as a genetic disease, cancer becomes a greater risk as the dog ages. Vets and dog owners have become increasingly aware of the threat of cancer to dogs. Statistics reveal that one dog in every five will develop cancer, the most common of which is skin cancer. Many cancers, including prostate, ovarian and breast cancer, can be avoided by spaying and neutering our dogs by the age of six months.

Early detection of cancer can save or extend a dog's life, so it is absolutely vital for owners to have their dogs examined by a qualified vet or oncologist immediately upon detection of any abnormality. Certain dietary guidelines have also proven to reduce the onset and spread of cancer. Foods based on fish rather than beef, due to the presence of Omega-3 fatty acids, are recommended. Other amino acids such as glutamine have significant benefits for canines, particularly those breeds that show a greater susceptibility to cancer.

Cancer management and treatments promise hope for future generations of canines. Since the disease is genetic, breeders should never breed a dog whose parents, grandparents and any related siblings have developed cancer. It is difficult to know whether to exclude an otherwise healthy dog from a breeding program, as the disease does not manifest itself until the dog's senior years.

RECOGNIZE CANCER WARNING SIGNS

Since early detection can possibly rescue your dog from becoming a cancer statistic, it is essential for owners to recognize the possible signs and seek the assistance of a qualified professional.

- Abnormal bumps or lumps that continue to grow
- Bleeding or discharge from any body cavity
- Persistent stiffness or lameness
- Recurrent sores or sores that do not heal
- Inappetence
- Breathing difficulties
- Weight loss
- Bad breath or odors
- General malaise and fatigue
- Eating and swallowing problems
- Difficulty urinating and defecating

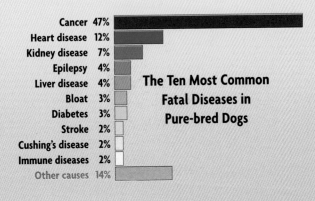

Cancer	47%
Heart disease	12%
Kidney disease	7%
Epilepsy	4%
Liver disease	4%
Bloat	3%
Diabetes	3%
Stroke	2%
Cushing's disease	2%
Immune diseases	2%
Other causes	14%

The Ten Most Common Fatal Diseases in Pure-bred Dogs

exams, routine tests and overall evaluations. Many veterinarians have special screening programs especially for senior dogs that can include a thorough physical exam; blood test to determine complete blood count; serum biochemistry test, which screens for liver, kidney and blood problems as well as cancer; urinalysis; and dental exams. With these tests, it can be determined whether your dog has any health problems; the results also establish a baseline for your pet against which future test results can be compared.

In addition to these tests, your vet may suggest additional testing, including an EKG, tests for glaucoma and other problems of the eye, chest x-rays, screening for tumors, blood pressure test, test for thyroid function and screening for parasites and reassessment of his preventive program. Your vet also will ask you questions about your dog's diet and activity level, what you feed and the amounts that you feed. This information, along with his evaluation of the dog's overall condition, will enable him to suggest proper dietary changes, if needed.

This may seem like quite a work-up for your pet, but veterinarians advise that older dogs need more frequent attention so that any health problems can be detected as early as possible. Serious conditions like kidney

disease, heart disease and cancer may not present outward symptoms, or the problem may go undetected if the symptoms are mistaken by owners as just part of the aging process.

There are some conditions more common in elderly dogs that are difficult to ignore. Cognitive dysfunction shares much in common with senility and Alzheimer's disease, and dogs are not immune. Dogs can become confused and/or disoriented, lose their house-training, have abnormal sleep-wake cycles and interact differently with their owners. Be heartened by the fact that, in some ways, there are more treatment options for dogs with cognitive dysfunction than for people with similar conditions. There is good evidence that continued stimulation in the form of games, play, training and

WHAT A RELIEF!
Much like young puppies, older dogs do not have as much control over their excretory functions as they do as non-seniors. Their muscle control fades and, as such, they cannot "hold it" for as long as they used to. This is easily remedied by additional trips outside. If your dog's sight is failing, have the yard well lit at night and/or lead him to his relief site on lead. Incontinence should be discussed with your vet.

exercise can help to maintain cognitive function. There are also medications (such as seligiline) and antioxidant-fortified senior diets that have been shown to be beneficial.

Cancer is also a condition more common in the elderly. Although lung cancer, which is a major killer in humans, is relatively rare in dogs, almost all of the cancers seen in people are also seen in pets. If pets are getting regular physical examinations, cancers are often detected early. There are a variety of cancer therapies available today, and many pets continue to live happy lives with appropriate treatment.

Degenerative joint disease, often referred to as arthritis, is another malady common to both elderly dogs and humans. A lifetime of wear and tear on joints and running around at play eventually takes its toll and results in stiffness and difficulty in getting around. As dogs live longer and healthier lives, it is natural that they should eventually feel some of the effects of aging. Once again, if regular veterinary care has been available, your pet should not have been carrying extra pounds all those years and wearing those joints out before their time. If your pet was unfortunate enough to inherit hip dysplasia, osteochondritis dissecans or any of the other developmental orthopedic

ACCIDENT ALERT!
Just as we puppy-proof our homes for the new member of the family, we must accident-proof our homes for the older dog. You want to create a safe environment in which the senior dog can get around easily and comfortably, with no dangers. A dog that slips and falls in old age is much more prone to injury than an adult, making accident prevention even more important. Likewise, dogs are more prone to falls in old age, as they do not have the same balance and coordination that they once had. Throw rugs on hardwood floors are slippery and pose a risk; even a throw rug on a carpeted surface can be an obstacle for the senior dog. Consider putting down non-slip surfaces or confining your dog to carpeted rooms only.

diseases, battling the onset of degenerative joint disease was probably a longstanding goal. In any case, there are now many effective remedies for managing degenerative joint disease and a number of remarkable surgeries as well.

Aside from the extra veterinary care, there is much you can do at home to keep your older dog in good condition. The dog's diet is an important factor. If your dog's appetite decreases, he will not be getting the nutrients he needs. He also will lose weight, which is unhealthy for a dog at a proper weight. Conversely, an older dog's metabolism is slower and he usually exercises less, but he should not be allowed to become obese. Obesity in an older dog is especially risky, because extra pounds mean extra stress on the body, increasing his vulnerability to heart disease. Additionally, the extra pounds make it harder for the dog to move about.

You should discuss age-related feeding changes with your vet. For a dog who has lost interest in food, it may be suggested to try some different types of food until you find something new that the dog likes. For an obese dog, a "light"-formula dog food or reducing food portions may be advised, along with exercise appropriate to his physical condition and energy level.

As for exercise, the senior dog should not be allowed to become a "couch potato" despite his old age. He may not be able to handle the morning run, long walks and vigorous games of fetch, but he still needs to get up and get moving. Keep up with your daily walks, but keep the distances shorter and let your dog set the pace. If he gets to the point where he's not up for walks, let him stroll around the yard. On the other hand, many dogs remain very active in their senior years, so base changes to the exercise program on your own individual dog and what he's capable of. Don't worry, your Bedlington Terrier will let you know when it's time to rest.

Keep up with your grooming routine as you always have. Be extra-diligent about checking the skin and coat for problems. Older dogs can experience thinning coats as a normal aging process, but they can also lose hair as a result of medical problems. Some thinning is normal, but patches of baldness or the loss of significant amounts of hair is not.

Hopefully, you've been regular with brushing your dog's teeth throughout his life. Healthy teeth directly affect overall good health. We already know that bacteria from gum infections can enter the dog's body through the damaged gums and travel to the organs. At a stage in life when his organs don't function as well as they used to, you don't want anything to put additional strain on them. Clean teeth also contribute to a healthy immune system. Offering the dental-type chews in addition to toothbrushing can help, as they remove plaque and tartar as the dog chews.

Along with the same good care you've given him all of his life, pay a little extra attention to your dog in his senior years and keep up with twice-yearly trips to the vet. The sooner a problem is uncovered, the greater the chances of a full recovery.

SHOWING YOUR
BEDLINGTON TERRIER

Is dog showing in your blood? Are you excited by the idea of gaiting your handsome Bedlington Terrier around the ring to the thunderous applause of an enthusiastic audience? Are you certain that your beloved Bedlington Terrier is flawless? You are not alone! Every loving owner thinks that his dog has no faults, or too few to mention. No matter how many times an owner reads the breed standard, he cannot find any faults in his aristocratic companion dog. If this sounds like you, and if you are considering entering your Bedlington Terrier in a dog show, here are some basic questions to ask yourself:

- Did you purchase a "show-quality" puppy from the breeder?
- Is your puppy at least six months of age?
- Does the puppy exhibit correct show type for his breed?
- Does your puppy have any disqualifying faults?
- Is your Bedlington Terrier registered with the American Kennel Club?
- How much time do you have to devote to training, grooming, conditioning and exhibiting your dog?

- Do you understand the rules and regulations of a dog show?
- Do you have time to learn how to show your dog properly?
- Do you have the financial resources to invest in showing your dog?
- Will you show the dog yourself or hire a professional handler?
- Do you have a vehicle that can accommodate your weekend trips to the dog shows?

Success in the show ring requires more than a pretty face, a waggy tail and a pocketful of liver. Even though dog shows can be

The bond between show dog and handler is a strong one, as success is truly a team effort. This Bedlington looks trustingly at his handler as if to say, "How are we doing?"

Not only the outward appearance of a dog but also the soundness of its structure is judged at a show.

exciting and enjoyable, the sport of conformation makes great demands on the exhibitors and the dogs. Winning exhibitors live for their dogs, devoting time and money to their dogs' presentation, conditioning and training. Very few novices, even those with good dogs, will find themselves in the winners' circle, though it does happen. Don't be disheartened, though. Every exhibitor began as a novice and worked his way up to the Group ring. It's the "working your way up" part that you must keep in mind.

MEETING THE IDEAL

The American Kennel Club defines a standard as: "A description of the ideal dog of each recognized breed, to serve as an ideal against which dogs are judged at shows." This "blueprint" is drawn up by the breed's recognized parent club, approved by a majority of its membership and then submitted to the AKC for approval. This is a complete departure from the way standards are handled in the UK, where all standards and changes are controlled by The Kennel Club.

Ch. Willow Wind Tenure, owned by Carol Greenwald, won the Terrier Group at the Westminster Kennel Club dog show in 2000.

Assuming that you have purchased a puppy of the correct type and quality for showing, let's begin to examine the world of showing and what's required to get started. Although the entry fee into a dog show is nominal, there are lots of other hidden costs involved with "finishing" your Bedlington Terrier, that is, making him a champion. Things like equipment, travel, training and conditioning all cost money. A more serious campaign will include fees for a professional handler, boarding, cross-country travel and advertising. Top-winning show dogs can represent a very considerable investment—

over $100,000 has been spent in campaigning some dogs. (The investment can be less, of course, for owners who don't use professional handlers.)

Many owners, on the other hand, enter their "average" Bedlington Terriers in dog shows for the fun and enjoyment of it. Dog showing makes an absorbing hobby, with many rewards for dogs and owners alike. If you're having fun, meeting other people who share your interests and enjoying the overall experience, you likely will catch the "bug." Once the dog-show bug bites, its effects can last a lifetime; it's certainly much better than a deer

judging the breed and in which ring the classes will be held. To start, Bedlington Terriers compete against other Bedlington Terriers, and the winner is selected as Best of Breed by the judge. This is the procedure for each breed. At a group show, all of the Best of Breed winners go on to compete for Group One (first place) in their respective groups. For example, all Best of Breed winners in a given group compete against each other; this is done for all seven groups. Finally, all seven group winners go head to head in the ring for the Best in Show award.

Practice and concentration pay off when the judge notices the professional performance of you and your Bedlington Terrier.

tick! Soon you will be envisioning yourself in the center ring at the Westminster Kennel Club Dog Show in New York City, competing for the prestigious Best in Show cup. This magical dog show is televised annually from Madison Square Garden, and the victorious dog becomes a celebrity overnight.

AKC CONFORMATION SHOWING

GETTING STARTED
Visiting a dog show as a spectator is a great place to start. Pick up the show catalog to find out what time your breed is being shown, who is

MEET THE AKC

The American Kennel Club is the main governing body of the dog sport in the United States. Founded in 1884, the AKC consists of 500 or more independent dog clubs plus 4,500 affiliated clubs, all of which follow the AKC rules and regulations. Additionally, the AKC maintains a registry for pure-bred dogs in the US and works to preserve the integrity of the sport and its continuation in the country. Over 1,000,000 dogs are registered each year, representing over 150 recognized breeds. There are over 15,000 competitive events held annually for which over 2,000,000 dogs enter to participate. Dogs compete to earn over 40 different titles, from Champion to Companion Dog to Master Agility Champion.

based on his merits in comparison to his breed standard, not in comparison to the other dogs in the ring. It is easier for judges to compare dogs of the same breed to decide which they think is the better specimen; in the Group and Best in Show ring, however, it is very difficult to compare one breed to another, like apples to oranges. Thus the dog's conformation to the breed standard—not to mention advertising dollars and good handling—is essential to success in conformation shows. The dog described in the standard (the standard for each AKC breed is written and approved by the breed's national parent club and then submitted to the AKC for approval) is the perfect dog of that breed, and breeders keep their eye on the standard when they choose

Accustoming your dog early in life to having his mouth handled while you clean his teeth pays off in the show ring as well.

What most spectators don't understand is the basic idea of conformation. A dog show is often referred as a "conformation" show. This means that the judge should decide how each dog stacks up (conforms) to the breed standard for his given breed: how well does this Bedlington Terrier conform to the ideal representative detailed in the standard? Ideally, this is what happens. In reality, however, this ideal often gets slighted as the judge compares Bedlington Terrier #1 to Bedlington Terrier #2. Again, the ideal is that each dog is judged

FIVE CLASSES AT SHOWS

At most AKC all-breed shows, there are five regular classes offered: Puppy, Novice, Bred-by-Exhibitor, American-bred and Open. The Puppy Class is usually divided as 6 to 9 months of age and 9 to 12 months of age. When deciding in which class to enter your dog, whether male or female, you must carefully check the show schedule to make sure that you have selected the right class. Depending on the age of the dog, its previous first-place wins and the sex of the dog, you must make the best choice. It is possible to enter a one-year-old dog who has not won sufficient first places in any of the non-Puppy Classes, though the competition is more intense the further you progress from the Puppy Class.

will be astonished by the many and different kinds of dog clubs in the country, with about 5,000 clubs holding events every year. Most clubs require that prospective new members present two letters of recommendation from existing members. Perhaps you've made some friends visiting a show held by a particular club and you would like to join that club. Dog clubs may specialize in a single breed, like a local or regional Bedlington Terrier club, or in a specific pursuit, such as obedience, tracking or earthdog tests. There are all-breed clubs for all dog enthusiasts; they sponsor special training days, seminars on topics like grooming or handling or lectures on breeding or canine genetics. There are also clubs that specialize in certain types of dogs, like terriers, hunting dogs, companion dogs, etc.

A parent club is the national organization, sanctioned by the AKC, which promotes and safeguards its breed in the country. The Bedlington Terrier Club of America was formed in 1932 and can be contacted on the Internet at www.bedlingtonamerica.com. The parent club holds an annual national specialty show, usually in a different city each year, in which many of the country's top dogs, handlers and breeders gather to compete. At a specialty show, only members of a single breed are invited to participate.

which dogs to breed, hoping to get closer and closer to the ideal with each litter.

Another good first step for the novice is to join a dog club. You

There are also group specialties, in which all members of a group are invited. For more information about dog clubs in your area, contact the AKC at www.akc.org on the Internet or write them at their Raleigh, NC address.

YOU'RE AT THE SHOW, NOW WHAT? You will fill out an entry form when you register for the show. You must decide and designate on the form in which class you will enter your puppy or adult dog. Remember that some classes are more competitive than others and have limitations based on age and win history. Hopefully you will not be in the first class of the day, so you can take some time watching exactly how the judge is conducting the ring. Notice how the handlers are "stacking" their dogs, meaning setting them up.

BECOMING A CHAMPION

An official AKC championship of record requires that a dog accumulate 15 points under three different judges, including two "majors" under different judges. Points are awarded based on the number of dogs entered into competition, varying from breed to breed and place to place. A win of three, four or five points is considered a "major." The AKC annually assigns a schedule of points to adjust for the variations that accompany a breed's popularity and the population of a given area.

Does the judge prefer the dogs to be facing one direction or another? Take special note as to how the judge is moving the dogs and how he is instructing the handlers. Is he moving them up and back, once or twice around, in a triangle?

If possible, you will want to get your number beforehand. Your assigned number must be attached as an armband or with a clip on your outer garment. Do not enter the ring without your number. The ring steward will usually call the exhibits in numerical order. If the exhibits are not called in order, you should strategically place your dog in the line. For

Here the judge evaluates a Bedlington Terrier on a raised table. With small dogs, a table is often used so that the judges can examine the dogs more easily.

instance, if your pup is small for his age, don't stand him next to a large entry; if your dog is reluctant to gait, get at the end of the line-up so that you don't interfere with the other dogs. The judge's first direction, usually, is for all of the handlers to "take the dogs around," which means that everyone gaits his dog around the periphery of the ring.

While you're in the ring, don't let yourself (or your dog) become distracted. Concentrate on your dog; he should have your full attention. Stack him in the best way possible. Teach him to free-stand while you hold a treat out

> **AKC GROUPS**
> For showing purposes, the American Kennel Club divides its recognized breeds into seven groups: Sporting Dogs, Hounds, Working Dogs, Terriers, Toys, Non-Sporting Dogs and Herding Dogs.

for him. Let him understand that he must hold this position for at least a minute before you reward him. Follow the judge's instructions and be aware of what the judge is doing. Don't frustrate the judge by not paying attention to his directions.

The judge looks over the line-up side-by-side to decide which of the Bedlingtons best conforms to the breed standard.

When your dog's turn to be judged arrives, keep him steady and calm. The judge will inspect the dog's bite and dentition, overall musculature and structure and, in a male dog, the testicles, which must completely descend into the scrotum. Likewise, the judge will take note of the dog's alertness and temperament. Aggressiveness is a disqualification in most breeds, and so is shyness. A dog must always be approachable by the judge, even if aloofness is one of the breed's characteristics. Once the judge has completed his hands-on inspection, he will instruct you to gait the dog. A dog's gait indicates to the judge that the dog is correctly constructed. Each breed standard describes the ideal gait for that breed. After the judge has inspected all of the dogs in the class in this manner, he will ask the entire class to gait together. He will make his final selections after one last look over the class.

Whether you win or lose, the only one disappointed will be you. Never let your dog know that he's not "the winner." Most important is that you reaffirm your dog's love of the game. Reward him for behaving properly and for being the handsome boy or pretty girl that he or she is.

After your first or second experience in the ring, you will know what things you need to work on. Go home, practice and

DRESS THE PART

It's a dog show, so don't forget your costume. Even though the show is about the dog, you also must play your role well. You have been cast as the "dog handler" and you must smartly dress the part. Solid colors make a nice complement to the dog's coat, but choose colors that contrast. You don't want to be wearing a solid color that blends mostly or entirely with the major or only color of your dog. Whether the show is indoors or out, you still must dress properly. You want the judge to perceive you as being professional, so polish, polish, polish! And don't forget to wear sensible shoes; remember, you have to gait around the ring with your dog.

Ch. Albee's Sunrise, handled by Carl Sanders to a Terrier Group win at Fort Worth Kennel Club in 1982 under judge Edd E. Bivin.

Ch. Vu-Pointe's Bianca, the top Bedlington Terrier of 1982, handled by Joe Waterman under judge Ann Stevenson.

have fun with your Bedlington Terrier. With some time and effort, you and your well-trained show dog could soon be standing in the winners' circle with a blue ribbon!

OTHER TYPES OF COMPETITION

In addition to conformation shows, the AKC holds a variety of other competitive events. Obedience trials, agility trials and tracking trials are open to all breeds, while hunting tests, field trials, lure coursing, herding tests and trials, earthdog tests and coonhound events are limited to specific breeds or groups of breeds. The Junior Showmanship program is offered to aspiring young handlers and their dogs,

and the Canine Good Citizen® Program is an all-around good-behavior test open to all dogs, pure-bred and mixed.

OBEDIENCE TRIALS

Mrs. Helen Whitehouse Walker, a Standard Poodle fancier, can be credited with introducing obedience trials to the United States. In the 1930s she designed a series of exercises based on those of the Associated Sheep, Police, Army Dog Society of Great Britain. These exercises were intended to evaluate the working relationship between dog and owner. Since those early days of the sport in the US, obedience trials have grown more and more popular, and now more than 2,000 trials each year attract over 100,000 dogs and their owners. Any dog registered with the AKC, regardless of neutering or other disqualifications that would

The Bedlington's natural athleticism shows as he flies through a tire jump at an agility trial.

preclude entry in conformation competition, can participate in obedience trials.

There are three levels of difficulty in obedience competition. The first (and easiest) level is the Novice, in which dogs can earn the Companion Dog (CD) title. The intermediate level is the Open level, in which the Companion Dog Excellent (CDX) title is awarded. The advanced level is the Utility level, in which dogs compete for the Utility Dog

(UD) title. Classes at each level are further divided into "A" and "B," with "A" for beginners and "B" for those with more experience. In order to win a title at a given level, a dog must earn three "legs." A "leg" is accomplished when a dog scores 170 or higher (200 is a perfect score). The scoring system gets a little trickier when you understand that a dog must score more than 50% of the points available for each exercise in order to actually earn the points. Available points for each exercise range between 20 and 40.

A dog must complete different exercises at each level of obedience. The Novice exercises are the easiest, with the Open and finally the Utility levels progressing in difficulty. Examples of Novice exercises are on- and off-lead heeling, a figure-8 pattern, performing a recall (or come), long sit, long down and standing for examination. In the Open level, the Novice-level exercises are required again, but this time without a leash and for longer durations. In addition, the dog

must clear a broad jump, retrieve over a jump and drop on recall. In the Utility level, the exercises are quite difficult, including executing basic commands based on hand signals, following a complex heeling pattern, locating articles based on scent discrimination and completing jumps at the handler's direction.

Once he's earned the UD title, a dog can go on to win the prestigious title of Utility Dog Excellent (UDX) by winning "legs" in ten shows. Additionally, Utility Dogs who win "legs" in Open B and Utility B earn points toward the lofty title of Obedience Trial Champion (OTCh.). Established in 1977 by the AKC, this title requires a dog to earn 100 points as well as three first places in a combination of Open B and Utility B classes under three different judges. The "brass ring" of obedience competition is the AKC's National Obedience Invitational. This is an exclusive competition for only the cream of the obedience crop. In order to qualify for the invitational, a dog must be ranked in either the top 25 all-breeds in obedience or in the top three for his breed in obedience. The title at stake here is that of National Obedience Champion (NOC).

RALLY OBEDIENCE
In 2005 the AKC began a new program called rally obedience,

ON THE MOVE

The truest test of a dog's proper structure is his gait, the way the dog moves. The American Kennel Club defines gait as "the pattern of footsteps at various rates of speed, each pattern distinguished by a particular rhythm and footfall." That the dog moves smoothly and effortlessly indicates to the judge that the dog's structure is well made. From the four-beat gallop, the fastest of canine gaits, to the high-lifting hackney gait, each breed varies in its correct gait; not every breed is expected to move in the same way. Each breed standard defines the correct gait for its breed and often identifies movement faults, such as toeing in, side-winding, over-reaching or crossing over.

The Bedlington's abilities give him the potential to star in agility competition. Agility is a "thinking" sport...plus, it's a great outlet for that terrier energy!

and soon this exciting obedience spin-off began sweeping the US. This is a less formal activity yet titles are awarded. There are four levels of competition: Novice, Advanced, Excellent and Advanced/Excellent. The dog and handler do a series of exercises designated by the judge and are timed. The handlers are encouraged to talk to their dogs as they work through the course. The judge evaluates each team on how well it executes one continuous performance over the whole course. The team works on its own as soon as the judge gives the order to begin. Handlers develop their own style in working with their dogs, using a combination of body language and hand signals as well as verbal commands. Faster and more accurate are desirable, though each team must work at its own pace. Signs are set up around the ring to indicate which exercise (or combination of exercises) is required at each point. Working closely around the course, the team heels from one sign to the next, performing the various exercises. There are 50 exercises to choose from, varying in complexity and difficulty.

Dog shows are social events as well, as everyone has one thing in common—a love of his breed. A group of exhibitors chat ringside as they await their turn with their Bedlingtons.

The dogs love this, and it shows by their animation and energy. Many of the dogs who participate in obedience or agility also do well in rally. While most of the first rally titles have gone to seasoned obedience dogs, it's encouraging that some newcomers have also earned awards. Rally is a good way for a beginner to start out in obedience. We hope that it will become a stepping stone to the obedience world and that we will see many more dogs and owners coming into the ring.

AGILITY TRIALS

Agility trials became sanctioned by the AKC in August 1994, when the first licensed agility trials were held. Since that time, agility certainly has grown in popularity by leaps and bounds, literally! The AKC allows all registered breeds (including Miscellaneous Class breeds) to participate, providing the dog is 12 months of age or older. Agility is designed so that the handler demonstrates how well the dog can work at his side. The handler directs his dog through, over, under and around an obstacle course that includes jumps, tires, the dog walk, weave poles, pipe tunnels, collapsed tunnels and more. While working his way through the course, the dog must keep one eye and ear on the handler and the rest of his body on the course. The handler runs along with the dog, giving verbal and hand signals to guide the dog through the course.

The first organization to promote agility trials in the US was the United States Dog Agility Association, Inc. (USDAA). Established in 1986, the USDAA sparked the formation of many member clubs around the country. To participate in USDAA trials, dogs must be at least 18 months of age.

The USDAA and AKC both offer titles to winning dogs, although the exercises and requirements of the two organizations differ. Agility Dog (AD), Advanced Agility Dog (AAD) and Master Agility Dog (MAD) are the titles offered by the USDAA, while the AKC offers Novice Agility (NA), Open Agility (OA), Agility Excellent (AX) and Master Agility Excellent (MX). Beyond these four AKC titles, dogs can win additional titles in "jumper" classes: Jumper with Weave Novice (NAJ), Open (OAJ) and Excellent (MXJ). The ultimate title in AKC agility is MACH, Master Agility Champion. Dogs can continue to add number designations to the MACH title, indicating how many times the dog has met the title's requirements (MACH1, MACH2 and so on).

Agility trials are a great way to keep your dog active, and they will keep you running, too! You should join a local agility club to learn more about the sport. These clubs offer sessions in which you can introduce your dog to the various obstacles as well as training classes to prepare him for competition. In no time, your dog will be climbing A-frames, crossing the dog walk and flying over hurdles, all with you right beside him. Your heart will leap every time your dog jumps through the hoop—and you'll be having just as much (if not more) fun!

EARTHDOG EVENTS

Earthdog trials are held for those breeds that were developed to "go to ground." These dogs were bred

---

THE CANINE OBSTACLE COURSE

Agility trials present dogs with an obstacle course, and these are the obstacles that are used in AKC agility trials:

• A-frame
• Bar jumps (one-bar, double-bar, triple-bar)
• Broad jump
• Dog walk
• Panel jump
• Pause table
• Seesaw
• Tire jump
• Tunnels (open and closed)
• Weave poles

Other types of jumps can be used also. The height specifications vary for each obstacle depending on the height of the dogs in competition. There are five height classes in AKC agility trials; dogs are classified according to height at withers.

JUNIOR SHOWMANSHIP

For budding dog handlers, ages 10 to 18 years, Junior Showmanship competitions are an excellent training ground for the next generation of dog professionals. Owning and caring for a dog are wonderful methods of teaching children responsibility, and Junior Showmanship builds upon that foundation. Juniors learn by grooming, handling and training their dogs, and the quality of a junior's presentation of the dog (and himself) is evaluated by a licensed judge. The junior can enter with any registered AKC dog to compete, including an Indefinite Listing Privilege, provided that the dog lives with him or a member of his family.

Junior Showmanship competitions are divided into two classes: Novice (for beginners) and Open (for juniors who have three first place wins in the Novice Class). The junior must run with the dog with the rest of the handlers and dogs, stack the dog for examination and individually gait the dog in a specific pattern. Juniors should practice with a handling class or an experienced handler before entering the Novice Class so that they recognize all the jargon that the judge may use.

A National Junior Organization was founded in 1997 to help promote the sport of dog showing among young people. The AKC also offers a Junior Scholarship for juniors who excel in the program.

to go down into badger and fox holes and bring out the quarry. Breeds including the Bedlington Terrier, Parson Russell Terrier, Dachshund and other short-legged hunters are used in this fashion. Earthdog trials test the dog in a simulated hunting situation in which trenches are dug and lined, usually with wood. The scent of a rat is laid in the trench, and the quarry is a caged rat at the end of the tunnel. The dog can see and smell the rat but cannot touch or harm the quarry in any way.

There are four levels in AKC earthdog trials. The first, Introduction to Quarry, is for beginners and uses a 10-foot tunnel. No title is awarded at this level. The Junior Earthdog (JE) title is awarded at the next level, which uses a 30-foot tunnel with three 90-degree turns. Two qualifying JE runs are required for a dog to earn the title. The next level, Senior Earthdog (SE), uses the same length tunnel and number of turns as in the JE level, but also has a false den and exit and requires the dog to come out of the tunnel when called. To try for the SE title, a dog must have at least his JE; the SE title requires three qualifying runs at this level. The most difficult of the earthdog tests, Master Earthdog (ME), again uses the 30-foot tunnel with three 90-degree turns, with a false entrance, exit and den. The dog is required to enter in the right place and, in this test, honor another working dog. The ME title requires four qualifying runs, and a dog must have earned his SE title to attempt the ME level.

CANINE FREESTYLE

One activity that is quickly gaining popularity and surely will have your dog wagging his tail, or in this case shaking his tail, is canine freestyle, or dog dancing. In freestyle a dog-and-handler team performs a choreographed dance routine to a musical composition of the team's choosing. This can be a fun and educational activity, as it incorporates traditional obedience training and allows the handler the freedom to integrate variations or invented steps and tricks that are not allowed in strict obedience showing. The dog and handler often dress in a style suited to the piece of music they have selected.

It is important that the dog's trainer be quite dedicated and skilled, as some breeds of dog are more difficult to train than others. Also, some moves in freestyle can put strain on the dog's joints, so be sure the dog is fully developed and in good health before beginning his dance regimen.

If freestyle seems to be an activity you and your Bedlington might be interested in, there are various organizations that hold freestyle shows. One such organization is the World Canine Freestyle Organization (WCFO), founded in 1999 by Patie Ventre. The WCFO holds numerous freestyle events each year, providing an opportunity for dogs to earn titles. There are member clubs throughout the United States, and more information can be found at the WCFO's website: www.worldcaninefreestyle.org.

CANINE GOOD CITIZEN® PROGRAM

Have you ever considered getting your dog "certified"? The AKC's Canine Good Citizen® Program affords your dog just that opportunity. Your dog shows that he is a well-behaved canine citizen, using the basic training and good manners you have taught him, by taking a series of ten tests that illustrate that he can behave properly at home, in a public place and around other dogs. The tests are administered by participating dog clubs, colleges, 4-H clubs, Scouts and other community groups and are open to all pure-bred and mixed-breed dogs. Upon passing the ten tests, the suffix CGC is then applied to your dog's name.

The ten tests are: 1. Accepting a friendly stranger; 2. Sitting politely for petting; 3. Appearance and grooming; 4. Walking on a lead; 5. Walking through a group of people; 6. Sit, down and stay on command; 7. Coming when called; 8. Meeting another dog; 9. Calm reaction to distractions; 10. Separation from owner.

INDEX

My Bedlington Terrier

PUT YOUR PUPPY'S FIRST PICTURE HERE

Dog's Name _____

Date _____ Photographer _____